Successful Product Development

Successful Product Development

Lessons from American and British firms

AXEL JOHNE

AND

PATRICIA SNELSON

Basil Blackwell

First published 1990

Basil Blackwell Ltd
108 Cowley Road, Oxford, OX4 1JF, UK

Basil Blackwell, Inc.
3 Cambridge Center
Cambridge, Massachusetts 02142, USA

British Library Cataloguing in Publication Data
A CIP catalogue record for this book is available from
the British Library.

Library of Congress Cataloging in Publication Data
Johne, Axel
Successful product development: Lessons from American and Brtish Firms
Axel Johne and Patricia Snelson.
p.   cm.
ISBN 0–631–17448–6
1. Product management.   I. Snelson, Patricia A.   II. Title.
HF5415.15.J64 1990
658.5'75—dc20   90–31256 CIP

Typeset in 11 on 13pt 'Monotype' Photina
by Butler & Tanner, Frome, Somerset
Printed in Great Britain by T. J. Press Ltd,
Padstow, Cornwall

Every product, no matter how adequate for yesterday's market, needs constant attention to keep it in the forefront of competition. Innovation – the development of new products and the processes to bring them to market – is increasingly a matter of fast and flexible response to change. At a time of intense global competition, none of us can afford to be too proud to learn from others' success.

JOHN BANHAM, *Director General,*
Confederation of British Industry.

Contents

Foreword

No manager today can afford to hide from technological and market changes. It is often an indication of the intrinsic health and vitality of an organization how it responds to change in developing and marketing its products. It is for this reason that so much attention is given today to organic growth, as opposed to growth by acquisition or merger.

This book considers business strategies and product management practices in large established firms. It differs from other books on the subject of product development by adopting an unashamedly marketing orientated approach. I personally welcome this orientation because it reflects my own philosophy of business. I was therefore pleased to see, although not surprised, that in the authors' sample the most successful firms approach product change from a market-led perspective. They do so on the basis of trying to capitalize not only on recent technological advances, nor solely by applying the latest market research techniques. Indeed, market research is often of limited use in identifying opportunities for really new products, as is explained well in later pages.

What distinguishes the approach of really successful product developer firms – and I am glad to claim that Amstrad is one of these – is that they deliberately choose from a range of opportunities available for making product changes. Put simply, successful innovator firms don't allow themselves to get locked into pursuing only one product development approach, which they stick with in the face of changing circumstances. Their approach is flexible.

The flexibility in approach stems from basing product developments on market opportunities, rather than on primarily technical possibilities. In my experience this provides far wider scope for improving product offerings than has traditionally been realized. As this book shows, fast-growing firms have in place organizational mechanisms for initiating or responding very quickly to changing market circumstances. Sometimes this will involve changing product features quite radically, but quite often it will involve making equally important parallel changes to the way existing products are offered so that they are made more attractive than those of competitors.

The authors give examples of innovative practices from large well-known companies such as ICI, Vickers, GEC, Plessey, Hawker-Siddeley and United Biscuits in Britain, and 3M, DuPont, Black & Decker, Kraft and Pillsbury in America. What I find exciting about the practices of innovative product developers is that they have learned how to destabilize markets by making appropriate changes to their product offerings at the right time.

Last, but not least, I am glad to see detailed discussion of an area of special interest to me: the role of marketing specialists. These are shown to have a critical role to play in product development. Unfortunately, contributions from marketing people often lack punch. This book shows why and how entrepreneurial vision of market opportunities can lead a firm to undertake product developments which will grow its business organically even when growth opportunities are seen as low by most others in an industry.

Skilful and effective product development is one of the most challenging strategic and operational issues facing managers today. It is true that product development will not automatically ensure higher profits. However, any firm which aims to grow profitably under its own steam must have products which customers will continue to buy despite changed circumstances. This is why managers need to pay such careful attention to developing their products skilfully and why this book should be on every marketing manager's desk.

DR ALAN SUGAR
Chairman and Managing Director
Amstrad PLC

Preface

FEW businesses can rely on yesterday's products to ensure continued competitive success. In recent years many firms have attempted to update their product ranges by merging with or acquiring other businesses. However, these routes are often risky and are becoming increasingly expensive.

Product development is an effective means for sustaining internal business growth providing it is managed skilfully. The interviews with managers in major American and British firms reported in this book show that successful product developer businesses listen to the market to discover their existing strengths before deciding how to improve old products and develop new ones. The findings show that market considerations must be the starting point for any effective program of product development. By adopting a skilful market-based approach the risks and financial expenditures involved can be reduced, often quite dramatically.

This book gives practical guidelines based on current successful management practice. A simple checklist allows managers to examine whether their current practices are suited to the type of new products currently under development. The book has been written for managers – product managers, marketing managers, R&D managers, new product managers, project leaders and business development executives – as well as academic students of marketing and product development.

Acknowledgements

OUR greatest debt is to our sponsor the Economic and Social Research Council, which provided the funding required to complete a field study, in Britain and the United States, of firms selected from four important sectors of the manufacturing industry. Not only did the Research Council provide the resources, but it also provided useful back-up. All the academic teams engaged in the program of research into the competitiveness of British industry met regularly under the chairmanship of Arthur Francis of Imperial College. The co-ordination meetings which were called allowed individual researchers to keep an eye on the broader picture whilst pursuing their own detailed investigations. The headquarters staff of the Research Council helped greatly too, particularly Dr John Malin who not only ensured that the study was set up in a businesslike manner in the first place, but who also helped in other constructive ways during its execution.

Every empirical study in the management field draws its greatest insights from information provided by practising managers. Our debt to the British and American managers who found time to talk with us is great. The book would not have been possible without their help and interest. We hope, therefore, that the conclusions and practical advice provided within these pages will be of direct use to them and also to their colleagues in the wider field of manufacturing industry. While it is impossible to acknowledge by name all persons who helped during the course of the study we would like to mention a few who provided particularly insightful information at the planning stage. These include Gary DiCamillo of Black & Decker, L. D. Metcalfe of Whirlpool, Jim Park of ICI, Don Duncan of DuPont, David Gustin of General Foods, Dennis Dick of Goodyear and Brendan Somerville of the National Association of [US] Manufacturers.

Introduction

THE United Kingdom Economic and Social Research Council launched in 1985 a £1.5m research programme into the competitiveness and regeneration of British industry. The intention was to examine issues within firms, within the control of management, which influence industrial performance. Empirical investigations were carried out by 28 different teams in various British universities, polytechnics, and other research institutes. Several related themes were pursued. These included the management of innovation, managing strategic change, the internationalization of business, the functioning of managerial labour markets, and the impact of design on competitiveness. Much of the most significant and substantial research findings have been written up as monographs for this series. Other results, and interim findings, have been published as various journal articles. A complete bibliography of output from the programme may be obtained from the programme coordinator at the Management School, Imperial College of Science, Technology and Medicine, London SW7 2PG.

In this book, Axel Johne and Patricia Snelson deal with product development in large firms in Britain and America. The authors show how established manufacturing firms in both countries have managed growth by means of internal product developments.

On the basis of a wide-ranging investigation in British and American manufacturing firms, some firms were found to be much more successful than others at achieving growth of this kind. The reasons for this are explored in detail and practical guidelines are provided on successful product change strategies.

Perhaps the most important finding of the study is that highly successful firms, both in Britain and in America, now actively pursue what the authors call **'market-based product development'**. This form of product change is quite different from traditional low-risk technology-led product improvement. The new approach relies on marrying market opportunities with what is technically feasible in order to achieve sustained competitive advantage. Market-based product development is now being used by more successful firms as a means for growing their business at a far faster rate than was previously thought possible.

The book will be of interest to all students of product development and especially to those practically involved, such as product managers, new product managers, project leaders and business development executives.

Its message is optimistic. It argues that despite the serious shakeout which has occurred in manufacturing industry, both in Britain and in America in the early 1980s, most firms can aim to grow through skilful product development. Sometimes this can be done with quite limited financial investment. It may, however, require unconventional approaches, such as subcontracting manufacturing. It requires not only determination, but a special mix of vision, commitment and skill on the part of managers at all levels in a business. A host of examples of relevant management practices is provided, together with a practical checklist which allows managers to audit current practices.

Arthur Francis
Series Editor
Imperial College, London

I

Background to the Study

THIS book is about one of the most important activities facing businesses. It deals with how manufacturing firms can improve their chances of winning the competitive game with newly developed products. It is not so much about *why* product innovation is important but concentrates on *how* product change can be managed effectively.

The last 20 years have seen a gradual domination of high-quality product development by certain Japanese and other Far Eastern suppliers. This has now become so established in the minds of consumers, as well as industrial buyers, that some electrical equipment in Britain is currently branded with Japanese sounding names like Matsui and Saisho but sourced from a variety of countries. Japan is now synonymous with innovation, customer orientation and high quality.

Yet, despite these changes, some British and American firms have maintained a constant record of achievement in product development. This book records the practical findings from discussions with such British and American manufacturers. It isolates success factors and points the way forward for those responsible for product development in their own organization.

We cannot stress too strongly the importance of the product development task in commercial organizations. It is the innovation of new products, their implementation and launch, and the change and development of existing products over time which gives a firm energy and vitality. Excellent product development *forces* a business to stay in touch with its customers and its markets, and *forces* it to look to the future. Our aim, through our research work and the writing of this book, is to give Western firms a framework to do just that.

In addition, we have identified relevant differences in culture and practice between British and American firms. It is not enough to ignore such differences, as they can play an important part in effecting the sort of results aimed for. To do so misses what is increasingly recognized as a key factor in corporate success, namely the ability to implement policies which prior analysis has revealed as being right, but which certain individuals may resist with all their strength.

A flavour of the findings

Our findings have led us to conclude that there is no one magic formula for successful product change. This is not really surprising, because product developments come in different forms. However, firms with a consistent record of high achievement in product development do tend to follow four guiding principles.

The first and most important finding is that high achiever firms make deliberate efforts to handle the two main types of product development in quite different ways. Amending an existing product is usually a much more straightforward task than developing a completely new product. Not only are different organizational arrangements used but the nature of top management involvement is quite different.

- Successful firms differentiate quite deliberately between the management of product improvements and the management of new product developments.

Second, we found in high achiever firms that top management does not distance itself from the inherently risky business of product development. In high achiever firms, top management leads from the front as far as product development is concerned. Having said this, it is important to stress that we found top management involves itself far more intimately in new product developments than it does in product improvements.

In the case of both types of developments, however, in high achiever firms, we found that top management provides the support and encouragement needed. We observed at first hand that, without guidance and support from the top, product development becomes a political game of push and shove from the ranks of middle and lower management with individuals seeking to act as champions.

- In successful firms, top management lends appropriate support to product developments which have been agreed as serving the needs of the business. Individual champions are rarely left to fight it out among themselves for resources.

Third, we found that high achiever firms are typified by effective teamwork. This means that once an overall product development strategy has been agreed, functional specialists are encouraged to co-operate as equals in the pursuit of broadly determined objectives.

- In successful firms, individuals from all levels are keen to join product development teams because these provide a vehicle not only for corporate growth but also for personal growth.

Fourth, high achiever firms look outwards at their present and potential markets and use the opportunities uncovered to drive their product development activities.

- In successful firms, product development is first and foremost market-based, not asset-based or capacity-based.

Selecting the firms

The aim of our research was to undertake a comparison of British and American product development practices across a range of firms. We decided to concentrate on large established firms because it is in these that there is a constant threat of inertia suppressing product change. Senior managers may, for example, have risen through the ranks by championing a product which they are reluctant to see dropped to make way for newer products. And, in large firms particularly, a multitude of reasons can usually be found for not doing something new, such as product development, which will almost certainly disturb established practices.

Additionally, large firms are very important in the British economy, accounting as they do for high proportions of employment and output.[1] While the growth of new small firms represents an exciting recent development in Britain, the contribution of large firms is likely to remain an essential feature of the national economy.

The main practical purpose of the research was to identify factors which inhibit large British firms from updating existing product lines and from developing completely new products for the purpose of competing in world markets. The comparison with American firms was considered useful because many American firms are commonly thought to be operating at the forefront of modern management practice, meaning that British firms can learn from them.

Deciding which British and American firms to include in the study caused much discussion at the beginning. We wanted the final results to be useful to a wide range of firms. This meant looking at practices in different industries. At the same time we knew that there are dangers in going too wide, because doing this means that one cannot hope to understand the operational problems of all firms included.

The final sample was confined to manufacturing firms in four important manufacturing sectors: mechanical engineering; electrical and electronic engineering; food and drink; and chemicals. Manufactured products still account for a substantial proportion of the Gross National Product in Britain and America. Further, manufacturing is an area which the House of Lords report from the Select Committee on Overseas Trade identified as needing special attention.[2] This report showed that Britain's industrial performance has continued to decline at a worrying rate. Indeed, over two decades imports of manufactured goods into Britain rose five times faster than exports. Not surprisingly, Britain's share of world trade has been halved during this period.

At the start of the study we thought that we would learn most by comparing high performing firms with lesser performing firms in the same industry sectors. We rejected this form of sample selection because pilot interviews revealed that growth performance commonly reflects the pursuit of distinctly different business strategies. For example, some firms have a preference for organic growth through internal product development, while others choose to grow through acquisition. This means that one will usually find well-honed product development procedures in firms which are growing by organic means, whereas firms which deliberately concentrate on acquisition growth may have in place only the most rudimentary product development procedures.

Further, in pilot interviews we found evidence of what some analysts have referred to as managing to a 'recipe theory'.[3] We found, for example, that firms in an industry often follow remarkably similar approaches or recipes for conducting their business. For these two reasons we decided to concentrate attention on comparing practices across industries rather than within industries. This decision allowed us to search for product development practices which have more general applicability.

Guidance in the choice of industry sectors, in which organic product development is being actively and continuously pursued at the present time and which therefore provide examples of current good practice, was obtained from a detailed in-depth study of currently published sources, such as Key Note Reports, Euromonitor, Mintel and Jordans.

We also contacted employer federations such as the Confederation of British Industry and the National Association of Manufacturers in the United States for advice. Trade associations were also contacted whenever possible. Useful insights were provided by staff of the National Economic Development Office in London. Other sources which were to point us to markets where product development is being actively pursued included analysts in stockbroking firms and editors of trade magazines.

After having identified industry sectors – or, more accurately product markets – in which product development is being actively pursued for competitive reasons, we made a determined effort, both in Britain and in America, to contact firms in these sectors that are successful in developing their products on a continuing basis. Because we were interested in practices in large established firms, Times 1000 companies, in the case of British firms, and Fortune 500 companies, in the case of American firms, were included. The British firms included firms like ICI, ICL, Plessey, GEC and Vickers; the American firms included 3M, DuPont, Pillsbury, Black & Decker, Kraft and others.

Focusing on the business unit

Large established firms have an ever attendant danger of bureaucratic procedures stifling innovation. Within such firms we focused analysis on the units which compete for business in specified product markets and which submit their own separate plans, budgets and reports to the corporate centre. In some firms such units are large and include a whole division; in others they are small and totally dedicated to competing in a particular market niche. We introduced a control whereby only those employing at least 200 persons were included.

We believe that the decision to focus analysis at the business level is important and necessary. We decided to do this after becoming increasingly irritated by generalized statements made about practices in large firms such as ICI or 3M which are made up of many divisions or businesses. These component businesses are often remarkably different, reflecting in large measure their operating circumstances.

For example, quite early in the fieldwork a visit was made in America to a business unit of a large multi-product firm with an outstanding reputation for innovation. A few minutes into the interview it became obvious that our respondent was not able to answer questions with the required accuracy and we pointed this out. In reply we were told that he was new in the post because the old top management of the division he represented had recently been replaced. On enquiring for reasons for the management reshuffle we were openly told:

Because the old team failed in the eyes of the corporate centre. It failed because they saw their job as running a cash-cow operation. Present day pressures require us to go for growth through innovation in order to retain our position as a major world player in this product market.

The fact that large firms have business units which perform with varying degrees of effectiveness comes as no surprise, but it does emphasize the need to focus analysis at the business level when market-related performance is being investigated. Hence, all examples given in this book are drawn from specific parts of large firms to illustrate current practices. Mostly the illustrative examples are of effective product development management. However, in certain instances less effective practices are shown to have occurred in some companies. The fact that this happens is not meant to slur the reputation of any of the firms mentioned. It merely shows that they, too, can improve.

The final sample

We eventually selected 20 British and 20 American firms to participate in the study. Many firms agreed to co-operate only on the basis of anonymity. In understanding and respecting this wish, it is not possible to provide a full listing of firms which finally co-operated in the investigation. Suffice it to say that the companies on which our findings are based are all large established firms which are household names in Britain and America.

Box 1.1 Markets sampled in Britain and America

● **Mechanical engineering**	● **Electrical engineering**
★ Mechanical handling	★ Test and measurement
★ Diesel engines	★ Office computing
★ Earth moving	★ Power hand tools
★ Machine tools	★ Telecommunications
★ Food processing	★ White goods
● Chemicals	● Food
★ Industrial plastics	★ Breakfast
★ Industrial rubber products	★ Dairy
★ Adhesives	★ Snack
★ Horticultural	★ Frozen
★ Industrial paint	★ Bread

The final selection of markets from which firms were drawn is shown in box 1.1. It will be noticed that certain important markets which one would expect to see represented within some of the industry sectors are missing. This was unavoidable: some markets proved difficult to access, in others a match was difficult to achieve because either a British or an American firm felt unable to co-operate.

When we do name firms it is to bring the substance of the investigation alive. It is not designed to heap gratuitous praise on certain firms whilst appearing to downgrade others. As will be seen, we have taken meticulous care to safeguard confidences and otherwise to protect sources. We do hope that any small irritation which might be felt by corporate personnel will be outweighed by the advantages of reading something with which they can associate more closely than is possible when firms are referred to anonymously as Companies A, B, C, D, etc.

Last, but not least, it needs to be mentioned that while British and American firms were the subject of the investigation, a number of leading Japanese businesses were also visited in the UK. These visits were valuable because they allowed us to check the rationale behind some of the product development practices in leading British and American businesses.

2

Product Development: the Strategic Choices

PRODUCT development is vital for the health of firms which want to grow by internal means. It is, of course, not the only way for a business to grow market share. Growth can also be achieved by acquiring other businesses, or by joint ventures, including factoring the products of others. These alternative strategies are not the concern of this book. Our focus is on organic growth.

There is an urgent practical need to learn more about the intricacies of product development. In recent years the pace of product change has accelerated considerably in manufacturing. It is only in a few basic extractive and commodity markets that heightened competition in terms of product change is not now an urgent and continuing consideration. Often the need for such change has been forced on a previously sleepy domestic industry by foreign competition. When home-based firms have failed to respond they have been wiped out or very seriously damaged, often in quite short periods of time – as has happened in both Britain and America in machine tools, motorcycles, consumer electronics, motor vehicles, and photographic and optical goods.

The effects of foreign competition forced restructuring across a wide range of manufacturing firms in Britain and America in the early 1980s. In many of the firms we visited, workforces had been cut drastically and sites closed in an effort to become leaner and fitter. Many firms also took the opportunity to rethink business strategies. Whereas in the past they had been able to go along much as before with heavy emphasis on improving existing products, many now need to stand up to aggressive and skilful foreign competitors who offer new products in quite new ways. It was competition from Japan which was mentioned time and time again as the driving force behind improving production methods and product offerings. It is now 'innovate or die' across a wide range of manu-facturing industries.

This chapter looks at the strategies behind product development, focusing particularly on a relatively recent *market-based* way of approaching product development. Our argument, in summary, is as follows.

- The traditional *asset-based* approach of simply building on existing product lines and technical know-how is no longer sufficient.
- Successful product developers look first at their actual and poten-tial markets. This guides them in determining appropriate *product offerings* for selected customers. It means that sales service, pro-motion, packaging, delivery and pricing are all seen to be as important as are inherent product performance features.
- Successful product developers look for an appropriate mix of competitive development strategies involving both line extensions and new product development, as well as careful cost reduction.
- Successful product developers ensure they understand and act on three major business factors:

  ★ The benefits looked for by their target customers.
  ★ The economics of their own supply system, and
  ★ The actual and potential reaction of competitors.

The traditional asset-based view

Traditionally, product development has been approached from the viewpoint of the supplier. A manufacturing firm will have existing products in its range and it may also be thinking in terms of developing new ones. These products can then be aimed at existing markets or at new markets, as is shown in table 2.1.

The simplest form of product development is **product cost-cutting** (1). In cost-cutting the aim is to maintain or increase profitability by trimming manufacturing costs while not detracting from per-formance qualities. This form of product development is important to nearly all manufacturing firms. Only when the pace of technological advance is so fast and furious that almost all emphasis goes on new product development can a firm ignore the need to continually trim manufacturing costs.

Table 2.1 The main types of product developments – an asset-based approach

	Product improvement	New product development
Existing markets (customers)	1 Product cost-cutting 2 Product modification	3 Product line extension 4 New product line
New markets (customers)	1a Product cost-cutting 2a Product modification	3a Product line extension 4a New product line

Product modification (2) is another option which is pursued by nearly all established manufacturing firms. Here the aim is to ensure that product features remain up to date in relation to those of competitors. In markets where there is an established set of suppliers, individual firms may take turns to make improvements. In other markets a dominant firm may lead consciously and continually in this respect.

Because these two forms of product development involve only existing products, they can be referred to as 'product improvement'. On the other hand, 'new product development' is concerned with product line extensions and with completely new product lines. New product development involves a business in developing new products of varying degrees of newness. For example, **product line extension** (3) represents a widening of a line of products already offered. Such products are also referred to as 'flankers', because their purpose is to strengthen an established product line.

New product lines (4) are products which a business has developed afresh. It matters not whether the type of product is already offered by another manufacturer (which is often the case). New product line development requires a business to engage in major internal changes. This is usually a complex and risky process, and is for this reason undertaken much more rarely than other forms of product innovation.

If a newly developed product line opens up a completely new market, it becomes an original **'new to the world'** product line. Such original product lines are rare. Examples are: video recorders, fax machines, personal computers, word processors, frozen complete meals, contact lenses, compact discs, mobile phones, personal programable organizers. They present opportunities for new product development to competitors who follow either as 'quick reactors', or as 'late reactors'.

The importance of potential markets

It is vital also to consider the market for which product developments are destined. Product developments can be aimed at an existing market or at a new market. Again this is an important choice for a business. In practice the choice made is often in favour of sticking with a known market because the risks can then be assessed more accurately. However, despite the higher attendant risks, much greater potential can lie with product development aimed at new markets.

The point of the above exposition is to stress that product development represents a rich mix of possibilities to a manufacturer, as is shown in Table 2.1. All too frequently, as we shall see later, manufacturers do not pay sufficient attention to exploiting the full span of opportunities. This is a common reason why some manufacturers fall behind. And, after a prolonged period of solely engaging in product improvement, a manufacturer may launch into a desperate program of new product development in an effort to make up for lost time. Not surprisingly, such emergency action frequently fails because of lack of experience in undertaking anything but product cost-cutting.

Market-based product development

We found evidence in many businesses which are growing really fast of a new approach to product development. Such businesses adopt more than an internal or asset-based view of business opportunities. They consider not only the newness of products and the newness of markets. The novelty of their approach lies in conceiving product development variants on the basis of *benefits* offered to *specific target markets*. This is quite different from concentrating attention on traditional product development inputs (such as technology for example).

As we shall show, the new approach presents manufacturers with a much wider range of competitive options. Businesses which practise the new competitive approach, either consciously or unconsciously, undertake what we shall refer to as 'market-based product development'.

The basis of the market-based approach is profitable exploitation of opportunities. It focuses on potential market opportunities outside a business – not on what the business has been doing up to now, or what it might do given its capabilities. As we shall see, it is a new and exciting approach to developing products which offers potentially much greater pay-offs than the conventional asset-based approaches.

The conceptual underpinnings of the market-based approach are to be found in fairly recent writings. Some commentators speak of the **'new competition'**, which is seen as being not between what companies produce in their factories, but between what they *add* to their factory output in the form of packaging, services, advertising, customer advice, financing, delivery arrangements, warehousing, and other things that add value.[1] In other words, it is not only the inherent quality of the product which gives it appeal, but other benefits associated with it.

Other writers have argued that as buyers gain familiarity with a product they find a manufacturer's support programs to be of declining value. In these circumstances buyers 'unbundle into components the products they once purchased as systems and open their doors to suppliers who sell on price and offer little in the way of product support'. The two American analysts, de Bruicker and Summe, continue: 'Even the most remote observer, once instructed, can spot this pattern'.[2]

These issues have been clarified further. Shiv Mathur, a professor at London's City University Business School, has shown how a manufacturer intent on maximizing competitive advantage may offer the same product to different markets, but can differentiate the product according to the level of support provided. Some buyers need a lot of advice (support) concerning the application of a product. Other buyers need less, and indeed in extreme cases may know more about the application of the products than the manufacturer. Hence, the level of support chosen needs to be appropriate to the needs of target customers.[3]

Market-based competitive strategies

Operationally the market-based competitive approach uses one of four differing strategies shown in figure 2.1. Two of these strategies rely heavily on product development for success. First a strategy which differentiates product *features* above all other attributes. This involves developing a better **product offering** (1).

The second strategy involves offering customers a 'tailor-made unique package' of product *features* plus special *support*. Like others, Mathur refers to this strategy as a **system offering** (2), because it permits customers to benefit from a whole amalgam of attributes. It occurs, for example, when customers are offered products with

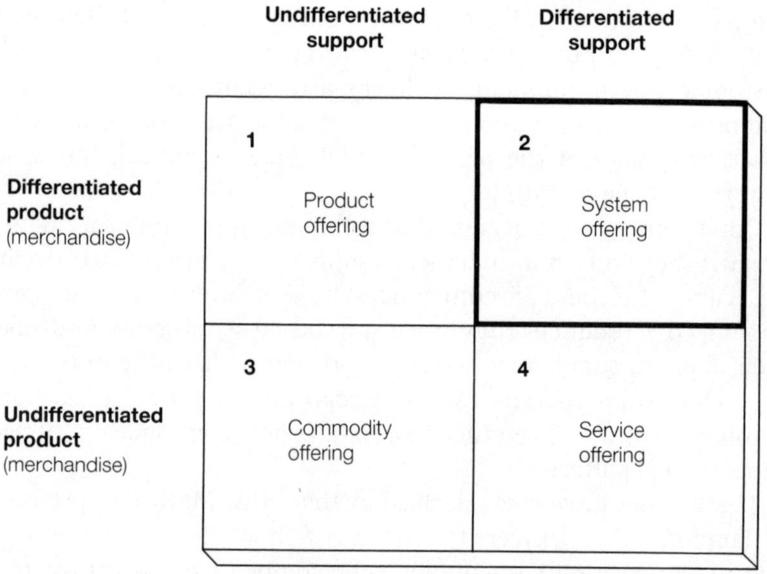

	Undifferentiated support	Differentiated support
Differentiated product (merchandise)	1 Product offering	2 System offering
Undifferentiated product (merchandise)	3 Commodity offering	4 Service offering

Figure 2.1:
A market-based approach to the main types of product offerings.
Source: Mathur, S. S. (1988) How firms compete: a new classification of generic strategies. *Journal of General Management,* 14 (1), 30–57.

support on how they might be best installed, operated, or serviced.

Of the other competitive strategies a **commodity offering** (3) relies first and foremost on *price* (because the product is offered without support and is undifferentiated from that of other suppliers).

A **service offering** (4) relies first and foremost on *advice* concerning how the produce can be used best.

Applying market-based competitive strategies

One of the most important findings from our study is that British and American businesses that are growing really fast by organic product development do, in fact, operationalize analytical concepts such as 'system offering' and 'commodity offering', and use these terms in internal debates. The approach used relies on taking a lead from the market with regard to the sort of benefits which appeal most to the prospects these firms want to do business with.

The approach is firmly grounded on the assumption that manufactured products are widely bought for a complex bundle of benefits. It is only in certain circumstances that products are bought solely for their intrinsic performance features, or solely as commodities. Many successful product developers are now spending as much (or more) on differentiating their *support*, as they are on differentiating their products.

For example, a well-known supplier of heat exchangers now offers the same basic product in different ways to different groups of customers. Customers that are well acquainted with the use of heat exchangers are sold to on a commodity basis. Such customers are charged the lowest prices in return for demanding no support in the form of application and usage advice. To stay competitive, the firm engages in product cost-cutting so that it can trim prices whenever this is needed.

The same firm sells the same heat exchangers to customers whose knowledge is such that it must be supplemented with support. Its customers receive detailed advice on how different heat exchangers can be used best and in consequence are charged a higher price. There is nothing really new in this. It is similar to paying more for a branded drink in a nightclub than in an ordinary bar. The product is the same, but the supplier puts emphasis on differentiating the offering by enhanced support for which certain groups of customers are prepared to pay extra. To stay competitive the firm supplying the heat exchangers constantly checks that not only the heat exchangers themselves, but also the support offered is as good as or superior to that of competitors. It realizes that it is the quality of the whole *system offering* which counts – not just the quality of the heat exchangers themselves.

If it is not able to differentiate itself in any other way, then classical product improvement and new product development will help the heat exchanger firm stay competitive. When doing so, however, the opportunities for scoring over competitors are much narrower than when trading on a system basis.

This example shows that product innovation needs to be approached from a consideration of the needs of the target group of customers. For operational purposes the message is:

- Be guided by the bundle of benefits which target customers are seeking and do not concentrate solely on the inherent quality of the product you are offering.

Understanding all the variables

Traditionally, manufacturers have concentrated attention heavily on enhancing product features. This is most pronounced in firms in which the technical department is given responsibility for product development. Interestingly, the situation is often not fundamentally different when responsibility for product development is in the hands of the marketing department. Marketing specialists also typically focus on those aspects they understand best and which are under their direct control. Not surprisingly, this has most commonly meant changing promotional expenditures.

What is missing from these narrow functional approaches to product development is a balanced and strategic consideration of the *total* span of variables which influence purchase behaviour in favour of the offering being purchased. When a manufacturing business begins to look at product development in terms of benefits needed by target customers, a very much wider range of competitive options presents itself.

It is well known that buyers form preferences for brands or makes of products, not only on perceived performance capabilities, nor solely on the basis of the image projected. A wider range of variables is commonly taken into account. For example, buyers of industrial products routinely take into consideration not only performance features, but also attributes such as price and delivery availability, as well as pre- and after-sales service. This whole mix or system of attributes makes up the product offering and will determine whether one brand is preferred above another.

For example, car manufacturers heavily stress, in addition to performance attributes, image and after-sales service. They have shown that it is the whole system making up the product offering which affects purchase decisions. It is, therefore, vital that this total system is the concern of product development efforts.

Some firms are now very skilled at this new competitive game and are putting into play a far wider range of offerings than before. Firms that have done this regularly consider fundamental questions such as

- Do we need to use the same channels of distribution as everyone else?

This question was asked and answered by Amstrad when this supplier of budget-priced computers decided to sell to businesses in Britain through high street retailers rather than direct. The decision reflected a move from a *system offering* towards a *commodity offering*.

- Do we need to go on promoting our products using a personal approach, or will a standardized product offered by direct mail generate better results?

This question was asked and answered positively by some banks that are now selling certain loans in this way (with predominant emphasis on the *product offering*). Traditionally, loans were negotiated personally through branch managers with most emphasis on the *system offering*.

It is this type of conceptual thinking which typifies the market-based approach. Adopting the new approach ensures that manufacturers do not solely consider performance features when choosing between product development options, but put into play a wider range of variables, which increases their chances of success.

Using a check-list for option choices

We found some highly successful product developer firms using check-lists to evaluate different product development options. These check-lists are usually made up of two sets of elements, as is shown in figure 2.2. First there is consideration of the *offering system*, which is concerned with attributes of importance to specific customer groups. This represents the start of the option choice process. There is, after all, no point in dreaming up new product concepts if these are unlikely to meet the preferences of target customers.

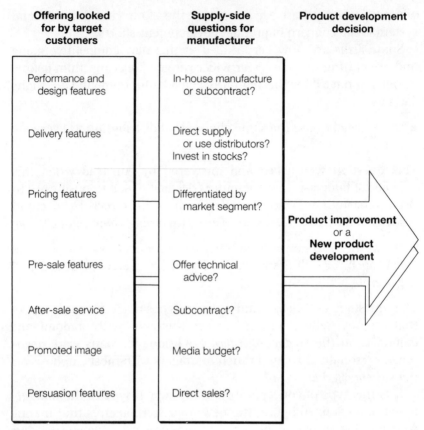

Figure 2.2:
Check-list for product development choices.

The offering system considers features that are likely to be important to customers in selecting one brand or product above another. These will commonly include performance features as well as other features which predispose buyers towards a particular brand. In the case of business customers, the benefits looked for can be teased out by undertaking an analysis of the customer's operation, as is shown in figure 2.3. This form of analysis is based on the value chain concept developed by Michael Porter, a professor at the Harvard Business School. He popularized the view that profitability results from the interaction of a number of interdependent operating vari-

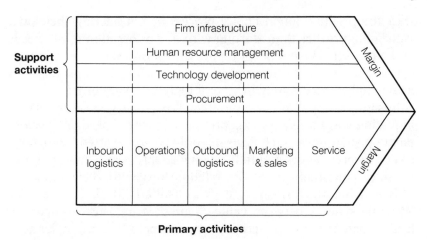

Figure 2.3:
The value chain for a manufacturing business.
Source: Porter, M. (1985) *Competitive Advantage: Creating and Sustaining Superior Performance,* London: Collier Macmillan.

ables. In terms of primary operations these variables include inbound logistics, operations, outbound logistics, marketing and service activities.[4]

Porter's analysis shows that, in addition to offering a low price, a supplier can offer other benefits to customers – most obviously those which improve their customers' inbound logistics and operations.

In the case of frequently purchased consumer goods, a similar analysis can be performed which will tease out to what extent availability and promoted image are important in relation to performance features. This sort of benefit analysis will reveal product development options appropriate to particular groups of customers.

The next step in using a check-list is to consider one's own supply system. This is undertaken to search for economies of scale which can be built on as far as one's own operations are concerned, as well as 'goodness of fit' with existing capabilities and resources. For each product development option it will then be possible to estimate likely resulting profits.

It has already been stressed that a manufacturer's supply system is of secondary importance to the bundle of benefits demanded by target customers. Despite this, many manufacturers still mistakenly start the product option choice process by considering their own value chain rather than starting with a consideration of the needs of the market. The check-list (figure 2.2) shows schematically how option choices can be determined. We saw such check-list methods being applied successfully in several high achieving firms.

It is interesting that we found some firms have gone even further in finding ways for identifying profitable potential product development opportunities. Such firms not only pay close attention to both customer preferences and to their own supply possibilities, but also consider potentially profitable relationships with their suppliers. This is what the British strategy consultant Mark O'Hare calls 'effecting synergy between value chains'.[5] Doing this can open up further opportunities for product development. For example, as is shown in figure 2.4, by purchasing fewer items in greater volume on a more regular basis, a firm may be able to offer its customers greatly improved product reliability and delivery.

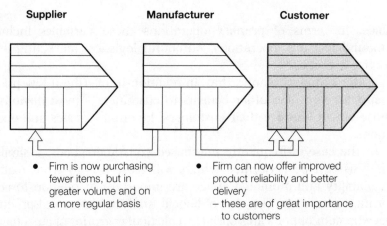

Figure 2.4:
Effecting synergy between value chains.
Source: O'Hare, M. (1988) *Innovate! How to Gain and Sustain Competitive Advantage.* Oxford: Basil Blackwell.

Selecting the most effective competitive option

Whichever type of product development option is chosen, it is important that it is managed not just in relation to customer needs, nor solely in relation to which option looks the most profitable from a supply point of view. A most important additional factor is the likely reaction of competitors.

Really successful product development does not just lead to extra sales volume, or to a temporary improvement in competitive position. Successful product development provides a manufacturer with defensible competitive advantage. Careful analysis of the competitive situation, therefore, provides another essential input for framing successful product development options, as is shown in figure 2.5.

We found that many leading product innovators are now very skilled at combining the results of analyses at the three operational levels shown in figure 2.5. First, they reflect explicitly on the sort of existing and emerging customer benefits which present opportunities for product development. The purpose of this is to clarify the way in which products will need to be offered to meet the preferences of customers in particular target groups.

Second, they undertake a careful analysis of three value chains: (1) those of their target customers, (2) their own, and (3) those of their suppliers. The purpose of this is to identify and build on possible synergies between these three sets of value chains.

Third, they undertake a careful analysis of the capabilities and preferred combative modes of competitors. Doing this allows them to gauge the likelihood of counter-attacks by competitors, both from within an established industry set, and also from a potential new set of competitors.

Conclusion

We shall see in the following chapters that high achiever firms, both in Britain and in America, use a far wider range of product development options than do lower achiever firms. This is the direct result of considering more options than do lower achievers. The reasons for this are not hard to find: lower achiever firms often

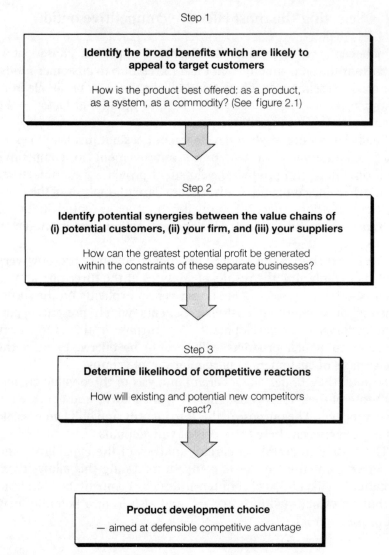

Figure 2.5:
Three essential steps in selecting product developments.

allow themselves to become locked into pursuing particular product development options which have never been systematically evaluated against a range of possible alternatives. At the extremes, lower achiever firms pay attention only to their operational assets when evaluating product development alternatives. Higher achievers, on the other hand, allow choices to be guided first and foremost by market considerations, and only after this analysis has been completed do they allow choices to be tempered by operational constraints.

3

How High Achievers Manage Product Change

IN the first chapter we explained the basis on which the sample of firms was selected. Forty firms were included: 20 British; 20 American. All were active product innovators to whom product development activity is important. Some of these were found to be highly successful at growing their business using this route and it is on these that attention is focused now.

The measure of success used to differentiate business performance was competitive sales growth. Our interest was in sales growth achieved through internal product development, not the type of sales growth which results from acquiring businesses or by undertaking joint ventures or by factoring products.

- A firm was classified as having achieved **high competitive sales growth** if domestic sales from a particular business had grown faster over the last three years in the stipulated product market than the sales of major competitors.

We asked firms to assess success in their home market because of difficulties in agreeing an acceptable definition of relevant world product markets.

We named such firms 'high achievers' to differentiate them from others whose performance had not been so successful. It should be added that we did not, quite deliberately, seek out newly established very fast-growing firms – the sort in which one finds product innovation pervading all operations. The aim was to study problems and opportunities for product change in large established manufacturing firms. Such firms have grown and prospered on the basis of developing yesterday's products and now have to safeguard their futures through continued product innovation.

Our high achiever businesses were found in a wide spread of product markets, as can be seen in table 3.1. An equal number of successful British and American businesses were selected deliberately for the purpose of comparison. The fact that equal numbers of successful businesses were included in the sample is not to suggest that either absolutely or proportionately there are as many businesses which are successful product developers in Britain as in America. Although we did not collect information on this, we believe that there are likely to be many more American businesses that are skilled and successful product innovators – on account of the much larger American corporate population alone.

Table 3.1   Product market location of high achiever businesses

Mechanical engineering manufacturing sector	US	UK	Electrical engineering manufacturing sector	US	UK
Mechanical handling			Test and measurement		+
Diesel engines	+		Business computing	+	+
Earth moving	+	+	Power hand tools	+	
Machine tools			Telecommunications	+	+
Food processing		+	White goods		
	2/5	2/5		3/5	3/5

Chemicals manufacturing sector	US	UK	Food manufacturing sector	US	UK
Industrial plastics	+	+	Breakfast		
Industrial rubber			Dairy		
Adhesives			Snack	+	+
Horticultural		+	Frozen	+	+
Industrial paint	+	+	Bread	+	
	2/5	3/5		3/5	2/5

High achievers in the British sample = 10/20
High achievers in the American sample = 10/20

Source: Field study findings.

The findings show that the majority of high achievers:

- have an *explicit* product development strategy;
- pursue a *proactive* competitive strategy;
- explore a *wide range* of product development options;
- have *formal* product planning procedures;
- distinguish themselves by using simultaneous *loose-tight* methods for managing product developments through which top management regularly checks the overall direction of intended

changes but allows teamworkers considerable latitude in completing specific tasks;

● use a *business-centred* organization structure rather than a functionally based one. By comparison, a smaller proportion of less successful businesses possessed this type of structure. As will be explained in this chapter, business-centred structures facilitate speedy and efficient product development.

For the purpose of achieving the research objectives, we decided on a purposive sample after it became evident during pilot interviews that large firms in both Britain and America face similar challenges and problems in managing product change. We illustrate the issues involved by comparing active product innovator businesses that are growing successfully with others that are less successful in this respect. Both national samples are analysed to show how strategies, plans and managerial practices in high achiever businesses differ from those in other, less successful, businesses. This also allows American practices to be compared with British ones.

What determines high competitive sales growth?

Analysis of current theories led us to conclude that high competitive sales growth is the outcome of a mix of strategic and operational factors. The task we set ourselves was to concentrate on factors under the direct control of management. We set out to test the extent to which product development success is the outcome of actions taken at two levels in a business, each of which is under the direct control of management. In broad terms, we hypothesized that successful competitive sales growth through internal product development will result when:

● a business adopts explicit strategies and plans; and
● a business skilfully manages the operational tasks involved in product development.

As far as the first general hypothesis is concerned, most analysts agree that it is important for policy makers to make explicit decisions which are communicated to those involved in implementing them. Accordingly, we concerned ourselves not just with content, but also with how strategic choices are translated into plans, including choices concerning organization structures.

The second hypothesis concerns actions taken at the operating level. Here we focused on the degrees of managerial skill shown within businesses on the part of those involved in carrying out operational activities.

Measuring the differences

In the field investigation all questions were focused on two operational issues: (1) strategic and organizational arrangements, and (2) management procedures. Because these issues deal with quite different aspects of managing, we made a determined effort to obtain answers from managers involved at appropriate managerial levels. In each firm, as a bare minimum, a policy maker was interviewed to gain insights into strategic and organizational issues. Additionally, whenever possible (and this was so in nearly all cases), an operating manager was interviewed to gain insights into current management procedures.

Capturing the complexities of management decision taking in the product development area is difficult. This is because product development comprises several distinct sub-activities. Luckily, however, there is now available a framework of analysis developed by the consulting firm McKinsey and popularized in the book *In Search of Excellence*[1] which provides a means for doing this (box 3.1). The framework was originally developed as a means for differentiating between excellent firms at the corporate level. However, because product development activities involve a very wide spread of persons and functions, the same basic framework can be used to investigate important tasks (such as product development) at the business level.

The McKinsey framework is also commonly referred to as the 7Ss framework. Its purpose is to capture essential management activities under seven headings, each of which begins with the letter S. Taken together, the seven factors provide a powerful insight into the way companies approach particular tasks, as we shall see.

Peters & Waterman, the authors of *In Search of Excellence*, go out of their way to stress that, in the past, analysts have paid greatest attention to the so-called 'hard' Ss of strategy and structure and

Box 3.1   The McKinsey 7Ss analytical framework*

The 'hard' Ss:
- **Strategy**   The plan leading to the allocation of resources
- **Structure**   The characteristics of the organization chart

The 'soft' Ss:
- **Staff**   The type of functional specialists employed
- **Skills**   The distinctive capabilities of key personnel
- **Systems**   The nature of the proceduralized control processes
- **Shared values**   The goals shared by organizational members
- **Style**   The cultural style of the organization

---

* Pascale and Athos[2] have also popularized the McKinsey 7S framework, but refer to systems, strategy and structure as 'hard' Ss. Peters and Waterman[3] refer to strategy and structure as 'hard' Ss. We have used Peters and Waterman's classification.

Source: Peters, T. J. and Waterman, R. H. (1982) *In Search of Excellence: Lessons from America's Best-Run Companies.* New York: Harper & Row.

much less to the 'softer' Ss of staff, skills, systems, shared values and style. The latter factors are referred to as 'softer' because they are far more difficult to quantify.

Each of the seven factors in the McKinsey framework shown in box 3.1 provides important analytical information on the workings of an organization. For example, it is important to know what sort of strategy is being pursued and also what structure is being used to implement it. These two Ss are the obvious direct responsibility of top management. Additionally, it is important to know what mix of functional specialists is used for particular tasks, what their skill base is, and what systems are in place to process work efficiently. Shared values and style – the last two Ss – are the most difficult to assess objectively, but Peters and Waterman claim that these can have a critical influence on performance, particularly at the operating level. We shall see later that these two factors do, indeed, have a particularly important influence.

The important point about the McKinsey 7Ss framework is not so much that all seven factors are critical, although they undoubtedly are in their own right, but that all seven factors need to interrelate functionally in order to achieve desired outputs.

We found the McKinsey 7Ss framework of enormous help as a means for diagnosing factors which are likely to be important in managing product development. For example, we used the framework at the outset of the research to ask preliminary questions (box 3.2). As far as the so-called 'hard' Ss are concerned we wanted to discover the extent to which high achiever businesses are guided by explicit strategies and plans, and the extent to which organization structures have moved from stressing functional inputs to stressing desired business outputs.

Box 3.2 Initial questions asked in the field (based on the McKinsey 7Ss analytical framework)

- **Strategy**   Is there a product development strategy which defines the sort of new products to be developed and the resources to be released for this purpose?
- **Structure**   What types of formal organization structures are used to implement product development activities?
- **Staff**   What types of functional specialists are there for executing product development tasks?
- **Skills**   What specialist knowledge and techniques are applied for executing product development tasks?
- **Systems**   What types of control and co-ordinating mechanisms are used for executing product development tasks?
- **Shared values**   Is there a shared belief in the need to pursue product development for the purpose of growing the business?
- **Style**   Does top management provide active support for those involved in key product development tasks and how does this support manifest itself?

Source: Field study questions: adapted from Pascale and Athos[2] and from Peters and Waterman.[3]

In parallel with such preliminary questioning we undertook a detailed analysis of the marketing, product innovation and business policy literatures.[4] Armed with the resulting practical and analytical insights we fixed on ten specific hypotheses which guided the main field investigation. Five of these hypotheses relate to the 'hard' Ss of strategy and structure, another five to the 'softer' Ss of staff, skills, systems, shared values and style, as is shown in boxes 3.3 and 3.4.

The main differences between high achiever and less successful businesses

In the remainder of this chapter we provide an overview of the findings as these relate to the hypothesis explained in boxes 3.3 and 3.4. It is important to state that as the investigation progressed we

Box 3.3 Hypotheses concerned with strategy and structure (so-called 'hard' Ss)

1 High achiever businesses are guided by explicit product development strategies. Less successful businesses have only implicit guidance on strategic direction.

2 High achiever businesses pursue proactive competitive strategies, that is to say, they will generally take the initiative in forcing competitive moves. Less successful businesses pursue less proactive, or even reactive competitive strategies.

3 High achiever businesses will pursue competitive strategies which involve a wider range of product development options than are pursued by less successful businesses.

4 High achiever businesses undertake formal product planning while less successful businesses undertake less formal planning procedures.

5 High achiever businesses adopt a business-centred organizational structure for effecting product developments. In less successful businesses the organizational structure is functionally based.

began to realize more and more that the ten hypotheses do not provide a complete insight into the intricacies of successful organic product development. However, they do provide a useful starting point from which one is then able to gain further important insights into a host of related issues. These issues are commented on in detail in later chapters.

For the purpose of presenting an overview, the managerial practices of high achievers are compared with those in less successful businesses. After these differences have been explained, we move on to consider differences between British and American firms. The reason for presenting results in this way is because the differences between high and lower achiever businesses are much greater, as will be shown, than the differences between British and American firms.

Findings concerning strategy and structure

1 *High achiever businesses are far more likely to pursue an explicit product development strategy than are the less successful businesses.*

As can be seen in table 3.2 nearly all (90 per cent) of the high achiever businesses in the sample embodied product development intentions in a formally written-down statement which guided the general direction of their efforts (eight British firms; ten American firms). Within the high achiever sample there was a marked pref-

Box 3.4 Hypotheses concerned with staff, skills, systems, shared values and style (so-called 'soft' Ss)

6 High achiever businesses use loose-tight **systems** for controlling and co-ordinating development work, that is to say, systems which allow for control *and* flexibility simultaneously. Less successful businesses adopt either predominantly loose *or* tight systems for this purpose.

7 High achiever businesses ensure that top management retains direct control over development work. In less successful businesses top management will not adopt such a supportive **style** of management.

8 High achiever businesses possess the requisite product development **skills**, particularly marketing and technical skills. Less successful businesses lack certain of the needed skills.

9 High achiever businesses involve a wider range of specialist development **staff**. Less successful businesses involve a narrower range of staff.

10 High achiever businesses have a chief executive who promotes a set of **shared values** which manifest themselves in corporate commitment to product change which ensures a supportive rather than combative environment. In less successful businesses the chief executive pays less attention to achieving a common set of shared values.

erence on the part of the American firms, as far as was revealed to us, to write down strategic intentions in elaborate and impressive looking planning documents.

As far as the less successful businesses are concerned, less than half (three British firms; six American firms) told us that they had an explicit written-down product development strategy. This is an important, although not necessarily a very surprising, finding. It suggests that businesses that are growing successfully through product development do so not by chance, but by deliberate intent, which is communicated to those involved. We found that, even among the less successful businesses, American firms are more prone to committing strategies to paper formally than is the case in British firms.

2 *Nearly all (90 per cent) of the high achiever businesses were pursuing a proactive approach to product development (eight British firms; ten American firms).*

Proactive means that as a general rule their expressed aim is to lead product changes ahead of their competitors rather than to follow. In the case of the lower achieving businesses the number pursuing a proactive product development strategy was much less: 65 per cent (six British firms; seven American firms). This is an important

Table 3.2 Overview of the main differences between high achievers and other businesses on strategy and structure

Hypothesis	High achievers		Lower achievers	
	British (10)	American (10)	British (10)	American (10)
1 Explicit (as opposed to implicit) product development *strategy*	8*	10	3	6
2 Proactive (as opposed to reactive) *strategic approach* to product development	8	10	6	7
3 Wide (as opposed to narrow) *range of product development strategies* being pursued	10	10	4	6
4 Formal (as opposed to informal) type of *product development planning*	10	10	6	10
5 Business focus (as opposed to a functional focus) in the *organization structure*	5	4	2	3

* To be read: 8 of the 10 British high achiever businesses pursued an explicit product development strategy.

Source: Field study findings.

result because it strongly suggests that success in organic product development is associated with setting out to exploit product development opportunities ahead of competitors. It is an issue to which we will return regularly in later chapters.

3 *A very important difference between high achiever and less successful businesses is the range of product development options being pursued.*

For the purposes of experiment, businesses were classified as pursuing a wide range of options if they are actively engaged in both product improvement and new product development. All high achiever businesses were found to be pursuing both product improvements and new product developments. Only half of the lower achiever businesses were found to be doing so (four British firms; six American firms). The differences between high achiever and lower achiever businesses were marked in this respect. However, as will be explained later, in the case of the most successful product developers, this represented only the tip of the differences in their choice of combative strategies. High achievers in product development now actively select from the very wide repertoire of competitive product development options which were considered in chapter 2.

4 *For product development planning, all high achiever businesses had in place regular and formal systems for monitoring products through their life cycles.*

In the case of less successful businesses the percentage was lower (six British firms; ten American firms). This represents an important difference in the case of British businesses, but not for the American businesses, in which there was clear evidence of a preference for more formalized procedures.

5 *Higher achiever businesses focus their organizational structures around outputs and not inputs.*

Organizational structures were to cause us much confusion during the earlier stages of the investigation because the organizational literature suggests numerous and often conflicting methods for categorizing formal structures. We finally adopted a relatively new method for classifying structures based on whether the organization structure is focused on business *outputs* as opposed to *inputs.*

We found that nearly half of the high achiever businesses in the sample had adopted formal structures that explicitly focus on business outputs rather than on functional inputs (five British firms; four American firms). A business-based organization structure is one which puts prime focus on business development above that of achieving primarily functional efficiency. The features of the relatively new business-centred organization structures are discussed in chapter 4.

We found the situation different in the case of lower achiever businesses. In these we found few which have adopted this modern form of organization structure (two British firms; three American firms). Those that have done so had a business focus imposed on them through recent restructuring exercises. On the basis of the evidence examined, it seems that when a firm adopts a business-centred organization structure it is far better able to address opportunities for growth. This issue is explored further in the next chapter.

We must add here, however, that all American businesses,

whether high achievers or lower achievers, had organizational arrangements which appeared far more orderly than those in most British firms. In some British businesses it was obvious that the organization structure had been built around individuals, rather than individuals having been found which fitted the organization.

Findings concerning staff, skills, systems, shared values and style

We turn now to differences between high achiever and lower achiever businesses at the operating level. At this level our concern is whether the two types of businesses actually manage product development tasks differently.

The results are listed in table 3.3. While we did find some important variations between high achiever and lower achiever businesses, it soon became evident that the original hypotheses (box 3.4) were unable on their own to explain differences in performance between the two groups of firms. Before turning to the hypotheses that caused special problems, we deal with those that provided particularly useful insights into product development.

6 *Clear evidence was found in high achiever businesses of loose-tight modes for controlling and co-ordinating tasks. Indeed, all high achiever businesses had loose-tight systems for managing.*

In these firms top management sets clear guidelines for progressing developments and checks periodically that progress is being made against predetermined goals. What happens in between is delegated to line managers who were given considerable freedom (looseness) to get things accomplished. Less than half of the lower achiever businesses (four British firms; five American firms) displayed any clear evidence of controlling and co-ordinating work in this way. The other low achiever businesses operated either in a predominantly loose or in a predominantly tight manner.

7 *In all high achiever businesses we found clear evidence that top management is prepared to 'front-up' product developments.*

That is to say, top management will assume full responsibility for product developments at critical decision points. This finding closely mirrors the findings concerning systems of operating. This is not surprising, because top management's style is likely to have a strong influence on the way product development tasks are administered.

Table 3.3 Overview of the main differences between high achievers and other businesses on staff, skills, systems, shared values, style

Hypothesis	High achievers		Lower achievers	
	British (10)	American (10)	British (10)	American (10)
6 Loose-tight (as opposed to either loose or tight) *systems* are used for controlling and co-ordinating tasks	10*	10	4	5
7 Direct (as opposed to indirect) top management *style* of involvement in development tasks	10	10	3	4
8 Trained (as opposed to *ad hoc*) *skills* are used for development tasks				
9 Wide (as opposed to narrow) range of functional specialists (*staff*) is used	Differences are a function of product development task (product improvement or new product development) *and* of activity stage – see text for details			
10 Multiple (as opposed to few) levels of management which participate in development tasks (indicating *shared values*)				

* To be read: 10 of the 10 British high achiever businesses displayed clear evidence of loose-tight systems for controlling and co-ordinating development tasks.
Source: Field study findings.

In only a third of the lower achiever businesses was there clear evidence of direct top management involvement in this way.

8–10 *Examining the hypotheses on skills, staff, and shared values caused considerable problems.*

For example, while we found very little evidence of formal skill training for product development in any firms in the sample, some lower achiever businesses had recently updated their product development skills in the face of competitive threats. This might lead one to conclude that the product development skills of the lower achievers are superior to those of the high achiever businesses, which would be an incorrect interpretation.

Detailed questioning of respondents suggested that differences concerning skills, staff and shared values can be appreciated only if one considers in detail the exact type of product development activity being undertaken. After all, product development does not occur instantaneously, but is the outcome of a number of essential tasks which involve different functional specialists.

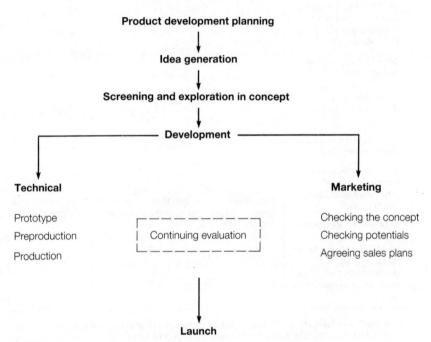

Figure 3.1:
Essential product development tasks.

Figure 3.1 provides an overview of the tasks involved. Product development tasks span planning; idea generation and concept exploration; screening; physical development; and launch. These represent the bare minimum of activities which need to be undertaken. For example, a business must undertake some form of planning so that resources used for current operations are diverted for development work. Ideas are needed for possible product developments. Some of these ideas need to be explored further in concept. As not all ideas for possible product developments can be worked on simultaneously, some screening out is required. Physical development and launch are obvious activities which are required for all product developments.

The five essential development tasks fall into two main activities: initiation activities and implementation activities. *Initiation activities* include all those tasks aimed at initiating product change, such as product planning, idea generation, concept development and exploration. *Implementation activities* include all tasks aimed at getting an actual development completed, for example technical and marketing development and launch.

Initiation activities

With regard to skills it is not surprising that we found a wider span of product development experience in successful businesses than in less successful businesses. However, this statement needs to be heavily qualified because businesses operating in different circumstances require different mixes of skills for initiation purposes. For example, in businesses which have so far *not* done much new product development, skills for artificially generating new product ideas may have been acquired recently at training seminars attended by key personnel. Yet businesses with a long record of product development usually have little need of artificial means for generating ideas: they normally have a bank of ideas ready for use when resources permit their further development.

It is not surprising, therefore, that in successful businesses we found greatest emphasis falling on the skills concerned with *selecting* ideas for possible development. These skills centre on exploring ideas in concept with regard to how a possible development might augment existing business strengths. This involves a far wider set of skills than has been traditionally invoked for product development idea generation, as will be seen later.

As far as the range of specialist staff involved during initiation tasks is concerned, high achiever businesses use a far wider range of staff than do less successful ones. The range was particularly wide for product improvement and somewhat narrower for new product development. This difference is important. Time and time again in high achiever businesses it was stressed that not all managers have the ability to envision really new products, hence there is a need to restrict the number of specialists involved in exploration activities.

The systems used to control and co-ordinate initiation activities in high achiever businesses are best described as 'loose' with no undue emphasis on regular and formal procedures. The purpose of this was described to us as avoiding the stifling of initiatives. On the other hand, many of the lower achiever businesses had very tight procedures for initiating product developments because, at the extreme, this was the only way to force through a certain minimum number of ideas for consideration. This was found to occur, particularly, when there was a dominant manufacturing and sales culture in a business which threatened to impede product developments.

We found that top management involves itself to different degrees in initiation activities. This is a reflection of top management's style in controlling specific activities. In high achiever businesses we found widespread evidence of direct control by top management through careful monitoring of ideas and the exploration of these ideas in concept on an informal basis. In such businesses top management's participation was not meddlesome. The purpose was to give support to all staff engaged in exploring concepts for possible product developments. In other words, the purpose was to engender shared values which stress the need to engage in product developments on a continuing basis aimed at ensuring growth for the business and for those working within it.

The situation in lower achiever businesses was often quite different. In these, top management sometimes distances itself from product development initiatives, in case they turn out to be failures. Top management's style for controlling product development work is frequently indirect, often through new product managers who are vested with heavy responsibilities but little authority. Not surprisingly, in such circumstances there is frequently a lack of shared values as far as product development endeavours are concerned. It is in such businesses that product champions are essential if any product development activity is going to be undertaken at all.

Sometimes there were obvious reasons for top management to distance itself from product development work. Most often this has to do with the need to watch the bottom line closely in the short run. On the other hand, in some lower achiever businesses we found evidence that top management is making heroic efforts to involve itself in the initiation of product developments. Unfortunately, in such cases, top management not infrequently suffers from lack of expertise in the rest of the organization: there being too few persons around with the skills needed for initiating appropriate product developments.

Implementation activities

Not surprisingly, it is skills above all other factors, which differentiate high achiever businesses from the lower achievers. The distinguishing skill of the high achievers is effective project teamwork. In these businesses project teamwork involves all functions contributing to physical development and launch activities. It is not merely intra-functional project teamwork. Some analysts have referred to parallel interfunctional project teamwork as the 'rugby' approach to development.[5] This is quite different from the traditional 'over the wall' approach where separate functional teams pass projects to each other.

It would be quite misleading to claim that all high achiever businesses have well-honed interfunctional teamwork practices. Many of these businesses are still in the process of working out the best way in which they can get specialists from different functions to co-operate. In less successful businesses there is, however, a widespread lack of interfunctional project teamwork. What often happens is that the responsibility for product change is located within one function (usually marketing or technical) which then has to negotiate and cajole other functions to co-operate. Often this causes considerable friction because the need is to enlist the help of persons over which marketing or technical specialists have no line authority.

High achiever businesses involve a wider range of functional specialists formally in physical development and also in launch activities than do less successful businesses. In addition to representatives of the technical and marketing functions, representatives from finance and manufacturing are also regularly involved. A distinguishing feature of all successful businesses is emphasis on involving a wide spread of functions in implementation activities. This is to achieve not only the most appropriate specialist skill inputs, but also to get commitment to what is being developed.

Less successful businesses involve, on average, fewer specialists from different functions. On average we found that the following three functions are regularly involved formally: marketing, technical, manufacturing. Few less successful businesses formally involve more than four functions during development work. Those that do, we found, are businesses that are now making determined efforts to change their development procedures.

The systems used to implement product developments in high achiever businesses are best described as 'tight'. After a proposal to pursue a particular development has been accepted, it is a matter of pursuing it efficiently. By tight we mean that progress is monitored formally using laid-down procedures. Following such procedures does not necessarily mean that progress is followed unswervingly. Built into procedures in successful firms are checks which are undertaken at development 'milestones'. If a development does not meet criteria laid down for a particular milestone, it is reappraised in accordance with the predetermined control and co-ordination system.

The situation in lower achiever businesses is usually quite different. Here loose systems for controlling and co-ordinating development work are often the order of the day. In some of these businesses, we found that developments assume a momentum of their own and have gone on for many years. There is a lack of tightness in the control and co-ordination systems used.

Top management's role is important in implementing product change. As in the case of initiation activities, top management in high achiever businesses involves itself directly. We found evidence of careful and detailed monitoring of development progress on the part of top management. The top management style adopted in successful businesses places great emphasis on direct feedback of progress. In some businesses this style of management is reinforced by 'wandering about'. In other businesses it is reinforced by means of an open-door policy. In all cases the aim is to convey and reinforce the impression to all involved in development work that top management cares about outcomes and that staff are supported in efforts directed at product change. Additionally, we found in high achiever businesses that the conflicts which inevitably occur during implementation are regularly resolved with reference to shared values. Open commitment to product change manifests itself in a willingness to resolve difficulties rather than to harbour unresolved problems.

Nevertheless, in those less successful businesses, where the chief executive is now taking determined steps to alter the way developments are undertaken, top management's involvement can be strikingly different. In such firms, top management is now prepared 'to lead from the front' as far as development work is concerned. We were frequently told that many chief executives like to involve themselves in the launch of important new products. Yet it is during the pre-launch physical development of such products that the direct interest of top management is of greatest operational importance, particularly by helping resolve conflicts so as to achieve speedy completion.

When the number of developments being pursued is very large, the chief executive may have to rely on systems for formally monitoring progress. It was stressed to us many times that what is important in this respect is for the head of the business to be *seen* to be involved. At best this involvement will not be meddlesome, but will reflect genuine interest and concern. All this was often lacking in the less successful businesses. Most of the chief executive's time was taken up on positional tasks – tasks concerning the running of the existing operation. Not surprisingly this negative message, as far as product change is concerned, was picked up by the very staff who could have done most to help develop new products.

Differences between British and American businesses

Although there are undoubtedly differences between British and American businesses it is the similarities between high achiever and lower achiever businesses in both countries which are far more striking and operationally important. Tables 3.4 and 3.5 provide an overview of the inter-country comparisons for the ten hypotheses which guided the investigation. It will be noticed that, for three hypotheses, it is not possible to provide a quick all-embracing overview of the findings. As noted before, this can only be done effectively within the context of a specific product development activity.

Differences between British and American firms result principally from the widespread preference on the part of American firms to formalize business strategies and operations.

• The first and by far the most striking difference between British and American firms is the greater emphasis on strategy, planning and control in American businesses (hypotheses 1 and 4).

Table 3.4 Summary of the main differences between British and American businesses on strategy and structure

Hypothesis	British businesses	American businesses	Important difference
1 Type of product development *strategy*			
High achievers	Explicit	Highly explicit	*
Lower achievers	Implicit	Explicit	*
2 *Strategic approach* to product development			
High achievers	Proactive	Proactive	
Lower achievers	Reactive	Reactive	
3 *Range* of product development *strategies* being pursued			
High achievers	Wide	Wide	
Lower achievers	Narrow	Narrow	
4 Type of product development *planning*			
High achievers	Formal	Very formal	*
Lower achievers	Informal	Formal	*
5 Basis of *organization structure* used for product development			
High achievers	Business focus	Business focus	
Lower achievers	Functional focus	Functional focus	

Source: Field study findings.

This emphasis was evident in all four industry sectors.

While we found, in high achiever British businesses, that product development strategies are often embraced in very general terms in internal planning documents, in successful American businesses such strategies were commonly laid down in great detail for the benefit of persons in the business and also for others outside it. For example, Cummins, the American diesel engine manufacturer even went as far as spelling out product development strategies in its annual reports. The annual report for 1986 indicates how far this firm is willing to take a wider constituency – particularly customers – into its confidence in this respect:

In last year's annual report we outlined three significant programs which reflect the impact of decisions made by the company since 1979. These decisions were in response to our conclusions that growth in Cummins' traditional markets had slowed for the foreseeable future, that overcapacity in world engine manufacturing would continue and that competition would be international in character. . . .

We have restructured the company into four business groups ... we have completed successfully the upgrading of our product line and the introduction of three new series of engines, the L10, B and C. We believe completion of this program gives us the most modern and technically advanced product line of any diesel engine producer. Product differentiation is the key to the success of an independent supplier, and we believe we have achieved this.

Such openness is certainly not undertaken solely in American businesses. In a successful British business, within ICL, we noted how written-down product development strategies are also openly discussed both inside and outside the firm. In fact, it was stressed to us strongly that great importance is attached to taking lead customers into the confidence of individual businesses for the purpose of framing product development strategies.

The preference on the part of American businesses for formal strategic planning was also very noticeable in American lower achiever businesses. While we found lower achiever British businesses typically pursuing a rudimentary implicit (spoken as opposed to explicitly written down) product development strategy, lower achiever American businesses were far more likely to have a formally written-down strategy that spells out implications for product development purposes.

- The second main difference between British and American businesses concerns skill inputs (hypothesis 8).

In this respect we were impressed with the sophisticated way in which certain American businesses are approaching product development opportunities. It was the intellectual effort applied in certain American high achiever businesses for the purpose of identifying profitable product development options which was especially impressive. These efforts are described in chapter 4. Not only were several senior managers in American businesses actively using sophisticated analytical concepts, such as Michael Porter's value chain[6] (discussed in chapter 2), but most managers using this type of schema were intent on taking it further within the context of their own business operations. In British companies we rarely came across senior managers who had acquainted themselves with

Table 3.5 Summary of the main differences between British and American businesses on staff, skills, systems, shared values, style

Hypothesis	British businesses	American businesses	Important difference
6 Management *systems* used for development work			
High achievers	Loose-tight	Loose-tight	
Lower achievers	Loose	Tight	*
7 Top management *style* of involvement in development tasks			
High achievers	Direct	Direct	
Lower achievers	Indirect	Indirect	
8 *Skills* used for development work			
High achievers			
Lower achievers			
9 Range of functional specialists used in development work (*staff*)	Differences are a function of product development task (product improvement or new product development) *and* of activity stage – see text		
High achievers			
Lower achievers			
10 Levels of management which participate in development tasks (indicating *shared values*)			
High achievers			
Lower achievers			

Source: Field study findings.

the latest management thinking on product development strategy and group working.

- The third main difference between British and American firms concerns management systems (hypothesis 6).

In lower achiever American businesses, product development systems were quite different from those in lower achiever British businesses. The preference on the part of American firms for formality in strategy setting and planning procedures has already been stressed.

Overall, we observed a marked preference in American firms for systematic or tight management procedures. In fact, in several lower achiever American businesses, managers expressed a strong desire for greater looseness in management systems: 'so that product innovations might stand a chance of winning through the stranglehold of laid-down procedures'.

In contrast, loose management systems for controlling and co-ordinating work were the order of the day in lower achiever British businesses. The effect was similar in operational terms: the product development efforts of many lower achiever British businesses were loosely controlled and co-ordinated, which meant that development times were longer than they need have been. As has already been mentioned, in lower achiever American businesses, tight management systems could impose a stranglehold on development progress.

Conclusion

The 7Ss framework developed by the American consulting firm McKinsey allowed us to tease out important managerial differences between the high achievers and lower achievers in product development. We found the framework particularly useful for this purpose because each of the seven factors represents an aspect of management which is important to and readily understood by managers.

Using the 7Ss framework did not permit us to comment satisfactorily on three of the ten hypotheses. This does not reflect inherent weaknesses in the framework. Much rather it highlights the need to consider the detailed environment in which each of the factors are operationalized. This, in itself, is an important finding, because it negates the notion that there is one 'right' way to manage product change. Because product change comes in different forms (principally as product improvement and as new product development), it is important that managerial systems are shaped to fit the type of product change being aimed for. This topic is developed further in the following chapters.

4

Top Management's Contribution

THE importance of the part played by top management in decision taking is widely recognized. There is a rich body of anecdotal evidence, both spoken and written, which stresses the importance of top management actions and participation. We were frequently told when visiting firms to enquire about factors contributing to business success: 'It depends so much on the person at the top'. Certainly, during our visits to British and American firms, we came to have more and more sympathy with this assertion, particularly as far as product development is concerned.

The published literature, too, stresses the importance of top management participation in decision making. A rich body of writings now exists on the critical role of corporate leaders. Not surprisingly, all recent major studies into product innovation management have shown that an important factor in bringing a new product to the marketplace successfully is top management support. Conversely, top management isolation from product development efforts, often stemming from a preoccupation with short-term business performance, is characteristic of failed innovation.[1]

For example, many commentators have argued that top managers need to have an open, imaginative and creative management style to encourage middle management innovators to function effectively. The American management consultants Booz, Allen & Hamilton have stressed that it is top management in innovative firms which provides the supportive environment for risk-taking and experimentation.[2] Such top level support is not a matter of direct hands-on control over projects. Studies have shown that over-meddling by top management can delay and upset the innovation process. Recently, two Japanese writers, Takeuchi and Nonaka have argued that top management needs to set the broad goals for innovation, but at the same time give the organization's change agents freedom to operate in fulfilling these goals.[3] This is what some analysts refer to as top management's role in 'envisioning, energizing and enabling the innovation program'.[4]

Our investigation has highlighted four main issues which together demonstrate the nature of top management's main contributions in high achieving firms:

- Encouraging and communicating a longer-term strategic vision for product change.
- Leading or following quickly as far as individual product developments are concerned.
- Selecting appropriate market-based product development strategies.
- Choosing appropriate organizational designs for facilitating product development work.

More specifically, our findings, which are explained in detail in this chapter, show the following results:

- The development and communication of a strategic *vision* is entirely the responsibility of top management.
- High achiever businesses tend to pursue a product development strategy which is supported by head office *strategic control* or *strategic planning*, in which longer-term objectives and pay-offs are accommodated. The 'short-termism' encouraged by the *financial control* strategy (by which subsidiaries essentially 'do their own thing' in order to hit increasingly tough profit targets) is not conducive to effective product development and long-term growth.
- Top managers in less successful organizations are both more secretive and less systematic in their product development strategies. High achievers almost always articulate their strategies in writing, and often make these known to their customers and shareholders in order to reinforce and to get general acceptance for the vision.
- Top management in high achiever businesses takes a proactive approach to product development. That is to say, they tend to lead or at least be early followers into a market.
- High achiever businesses set out to grow new market demand –

not just compete harder for a bigger share of an established market.

- High achiever businesses engage constantly in both product improvement and also new product development. Less successful businesses may concentrate on one or the other.
- High achiever businesses have moved/are moving to a business-based organization design (away from a purely function-based one). In high achiever businesses, top management creates and nurtures cross-functional market-led product development teams.

Encouraging and communicating vision

In large multi-product firms, top management can exert influence over product developments from two vantage points. First, from the corporate centre; second, from the chief executive of an operating division or strategic business unit. Both are important. The way the corporate centre can exert influence over constituent businesses is illustrated well in the 1986 annual report for Campbell, a leading American food manufacturer:

When R. Gordon McGovern took the helm in October 1980 the basic organization structure consisted of three major operating divisions based on very broad product lines. That arrangement was appropriate in earlier days ... [but] the centralized organizational chain of command threatened to impede growth. So management decided to decentralize operations. To-day there are some 50 separate business units. Each of the general managers of these units has responsibility for the product category, and for carrying new products all the way from idea to the marketplace.

Without guidance and support from the top, autonomy can quickly turn into chaos. [Top] management bears the ultimate responsibility for overseeing all the 'businesses within the business'.

However laudable the above sentiments sound, it must be accepted that not all corporations choose to run their businesses in this manner. Different approaches or styles for managing constituent parts of large corporations have been admirably analysed by two British academics, Goold and Campbell.[5] These researchers have identified three main styles:

- Strategic control or 'coaching'

- Strategic planning or 'orchestrating'
- Financial control

The style of the food manufacturer Campbell is one of controlling its offspring strategically. Such a *strategic control* style is practised in Britain by firms such as Courtaulds, ICI, Plessey and Vickers. Under the strategic control style, the centre prefers to leave the initiative in the development of plans to business unit managers. But, the centre reviews and criticizes plans (through 'coaching'), and uses the reviews as a check on the quality of thinking on the part of business unit managers.

Corporations which practise a *strategic planning* style give less autonomy to individual businesses because the corporate centre involves itself intimately in framing or 'orchestrating' policies for constituent parts. This style is practised in Britain by firms such as BOC, BP, Cadbury Schweppes, Lex, STC and United Biscuits. Within strategic planning companies, the centre works with business unit managers to develop strategy. For this purpose, the centre establishes extensive planning procedures. It also seeks to make important contributions to strategic thinking, for which the company will probably have an explicit overall corporate strategy (or mission statement) which is used to co-ordinate and control developments across different businesses.

On the other hand, in *financial control* companies, the corporate centre involves itself hardly at all in steering offspring strategically, preferring to concentrate on monitoring financial performance. In Britain, examples of financial control companies are BTR, Ferranti, GEC, Hanson Trust and Tarmac.

The way in which corporate control is exercised is likely to have a direct bearing on the level and effectiveness of product development efforts in the firm as a whole, as well as within individual divisions or strategic business units. Product development – of whatever type – costs money, and only generates revenue in the longer term. In such circumstances, it is clear that a financial control style, in which individual businesses are required to generate a high level of current earnings, will usually militate against product development efforts.

The following statement by the R&D director of a British electrical engineering business illustrates how the financial control style can discourage product development:

Of course we should have been investing in product development, but we didn't . . . . In the past the emphasis has always been on current financial results, so not surprisingly it was very difficult for me to persuade the chief executive [of the business] to release funds for projects which were unlikely to pay off for several years. We knew at the time that it was not serving the best interests of the business in the long run, but we had to accept that it was short-term considerations, particularly very short pay-back expectations from head office, which dominated our thinking.

Strategic control style

Less obviously damaging is the corporate pursuit of 'organizational decentralization' which represents an effort to get individual businesses closer to their marketplaces. However, often this approach is not supported by financial policies which are flexible enough to allow businesses to meet the investment demands of product change whilst enabling the corporate centre to control overall profitability. This problem is illustrated by the comments of a manager in a major UK food products firm:

At the moment, product development is done within a particular business. But this means that the General Managers (of each of the businesses) carry all the risks, which has tended to make them more conservative than is good for their business. So we are thinking of making funds available centrally for which General Managers can apply. We see our main problem at the moment as being to give effective support so that businesses can be rejuvenated.

While such decentralization provides the potential for individual businesses to get closer to their current marketplaces, it offers little which will enable the firm as a whole to understand the total market environment in which new business opportunities continually evolve. For this purpose, a firm needs the ability to envision long-term business opportunities alongside developing and understanding the dynamics of current market trends. The role of top management in facilitating both these strategic needs is of obvious critical importance.

Strategic planning style

In the American firm DuPont, which practises a predominantly strategic planning style, we came across an effective means for reconciling both short-term profitability needs with longer-term product development demands. Within certain divisions of DuPont, top management has introduced monthly 'strategic reassessment reviews' which run parallel to, but are separate from, the traditional regular profit and loss presentations by business unit heads. By this means the manager responsible for a particular business is in a position to argue that while his bottom line may not be spectacular in the short run, he needs to continue to invest resources in order to safeguard the long-term future of his business. A director of planning in one of DuPont's divisions summed up the mode of operation neatly:

At these meetings my job [as right hand man to the CEO] is to ensure that there is a proper strategic assessment in relation to the whole division's strengths, weaknesses, threats and opportunities as well as to see that the managers of individual businesses are not just intent on building up an empire for themselves. If a business manager feels that we are being unfair, he can always go direct and make an appeal to the head of the division. All this has to be done within a vision of how the division can best position itself to compete in 10 to 15 years time. In other words, which markets should we be in with what sort of products?

Vision

The importance of vision for the purpose of competing effectively in the longer run was stressed in many high achieving businesses. Time and time again respondents emphasized that relatively few persons in a business are capable of, or have the time to develop such strategic visions of the future. Clearly, the development of a total business vision is the responsibility of top management: it is top management which has, or should have, the personal abilities to conceptualize a strategic direction for the overall business. It is this vision which, if successfully communicated, attracts the necessary following from all other organizational participants. A director responsible for product and business development in General Foods summed up the issues in the following terms:

Established product lines can be run on straightforward planning. New developments run on belief. An essential ingredient of successful new product development is vision. Vision expressed in such a way that it connects with peoples' sense of purpose. The way you get high performance from people is when they feel that their personal aims are linked with the aims of the business.

Top management must provide that vision and support it with resources. If top management does not provide a vision, or at least provides clear support for a vision, you no longer have the conditions necessary for effective team performance. When top management does not provide such support it is in effect saying: 'what you are doing is not worthwhile'. When this happens, people retreat into being functional specialists. There is nothing to hold them together as a team.

The way to get peak performance is to fire-up people. In that way you often get them to perform far above what was thought possible. That's why top management's contribution to product development is so important.

The CEO as rejuvenator

That an organization's strategic thrust is engineered by the activities and influence of top management is clear from the number of instances where corporate rejuvenation has coincided with an infusion of new blood at the top. What happened in the case of the American firm Whirlpool was not unusual in this respect. Until chief executive Jack Sparks took over in 1982 the corporation had operated more like a bank than a manufacturing firm. In fact, the corporation was reported to be making a greater return from its accumulated cash mountain than from manufacturing domestic appliances. The situation was apparently extremely unhealthy, as is illustrated by comments made to us by a technical manager of the company:

Until Mr Sparks took the helm we were a money machine. It wasn't entirely surprising because the previous CEO was a finance specialist. We spent little on R&D. The emphasis was on reducing costs. We made money – lots of it – but it was being made indirectly. Not through the business . . . . We were allowing our products to turn into commodities. If the trend had not been reversed we probably would not be in business now, and we certainly would not be a world player.

The catalyst for rejuvenation is top management's willingness to envision the way forward. The means by which such a vision is translated into reality will be reflected in the way top management articulates its vision into clear strategic directives. Whirlpool's then new chief executive spelled out his vision for the company by stressing five objectives:

- Profitability
- Quality
- Growth of the business
- Human resources – to be a responsible employer
- Innovation – mainly product innovation

Main board directors were made responsible for working towards each of these objectives. The objectives were reinforced again at the divisional level by making specific individuals responsible for performance in each one of the five areas. Interestingly, the focus provided by the new direction began to pay dividends in terms of increased operating profits after three years.

Growth objectives with specific guidelines

In successful British businesses we found similar evidence of emphasis by top management at the corporate centre on growth objectives, as well as specific guidelines on how these are to be achieved. In ICI, for example, under the new chairmanship of John Harvey-Jones, the old product-based divisional structure was replaced by a business-centred organization.[6] Each major business, as in the case of Whirlpool, was required to pay detailed attention to a manageable number of output objectives and to appoint a director with responsibility for these. The purpose in spelling out these responsibilities was to develop and grow chosen businesses by fusing the efforts of separate specialists.

Similar transformations have occurred across a wide spectrum of British manufacturing industry. In the British computer manufacturer ICL, for example, a cultural revolution took place in the early 1980s. The old ICL was technology led. It had a poor grasp of marketing and lacked clear strategic direction. Like ICI, ICL was transformed, by a new chairman, from a functionally specialized company into a business-centred company. To reinforce structural changes, 'Way-Ahead' briefings were held regularly for all staff, so that the new strategic direction could be spelled out and explained. And, at ICL, it was emphasized to us that the explaining of product development strategies did not stop internally. The company involved all participants in the value chain, including customers and suppliers.

In high achieving businesses, communication of the strategic thrust for product change is frequently underpinned by detailed written product strategies and plans backed up by regular staff briefings. American firms, in particular, place great emphasis on communicating product development strategies all the way through the organization. For this purpose regular briefing meetings are held, usually annually. But when the pace of change in an industry is particularly fast, we found that such meetings are held more frequently. This also occurs in British firms. For example, top management in constituent businesses belonging to Vickers are encouraged to hold monthly briefing sessions with staff for this purpose. It is at such regular briefings that development strategies for particular product lines are spelled-out.

On the basis of what we observed in high achiever businesses and also what was stressed to us by many persons in less successful product developer businesses, top management has a most important role to play in explaining the intended direction for product change. We found great emphasis on this in firms on both sides of the Atlantic. Even in businesses in which product development performance is at present below par, we found evidence of increasing acceptance for more open communication about intended development strategies.

Less successful businesses

It was, however, somewhat exceptional for the senior managers in less successful businesses to be really open in their communications concerning product change. In the main, we found that top management in these prefer to play their cards very close to the chest. In large part this appears to stem from top management's preference for managing in a way which requires little explanation. Often, this style of managing rested on tradition, as was explained by a marketing manager in a British bakery business:

Our industry has traditionally never given much credence to long-term strategic thinking. It is a daily business we are in, rather like newspapers. This short-term culture has pervaded all management levels. As a result, there has not been much strategic thinking. My task is to change this, but I can tell you it's an uphill battle.

It is worth commenting that the person making this statement was not a member of his firm's executive board which was made up of solely production and sales personnel. Marketing in his firm was a staff advisory function. We return to the implications for product development of this type of organizational arrangement a little later in the chapter.

Lack of an explicit written-down product development strategy differentiated clearly between high achievers and less successful product developer businesses. It is important to stress, however, that many businesses are now taking urgent steps to rectify this situation, as was illustrated by the managing director of a British horticultural products business:

We don't have a formal written-down product development strategy. We are working on this right now. At the moment our implicit strategy is to stay in our area of sales.

To lead or to follow?

The adjective which best describes high achiever businesses is 'proactive'. Their strategic approach is to go forward confidently, most usually ahead of the competition, on the basis of a careful reading of market opportunities. We want to stress that a proactive approach does not necessarily imply always being the first to the market. Rather, it involves taking the lead in understanding and responding to market developments, as was illustrated by a senior manager in the American firm Black & Decker:

The closer you stay with your present products or markets the safer the product development game is. You either want to be in the game or not. Product development as an aggressive strategy is not for everyone. Most Far Eastern companies – with the exception of the best Japanese firms – are specialists in manufacturing. They go after manufacturing innovation.

We, however, want to be leading product innovators. It is true that we could probably survive as a quick follower – or as a fast second – because of our marketing and distribution strengths. But we have decided to grow the company through product innovation – particularly by adding higher value products.

The managing director of a fairly recently established new business in the British firm Bowater also provides insights into the nature of the proactive approach, by comparing his company's vision of the marketplace with that held by his competitors:

Our product development is market led. It has been from the start. We are most definitely not committed to our manufacturing technology. If a better technology comes along, we will junk the plant. It's been paid for. We would invest in new technology.

Our approach is fundamentally different. I notice that particularly when I meet my competitors at trade association meetings. It's very interesting ... it's obvious that they are switched into a different mind-set from us. They see the market growing very slowly, but then they are looking for steady growth from traditional product lines.

We, on the other hand, have grown from 8 per cent to 50 per cent of our chosen part of the bulk packaging market in six years, and we've done it without stealing any business from the traditional competitors! What we are doing is enlarging the size of the total cake by helping chosen customers [who need better fertilizer packaging] to do better in their chosen markets. But it's us who have taken the lead in opening up a whole new market.

Contrasting sharply with these proactive, market-led, approaches to product development, consider the views expressed by the R&D Director of a less successful British engineering business:

Our competitors are forcing the pace of change with a maximum life for any product now becoming five years.... If I were trying to give you the formal line I would say: 'of course the business is market-led in its product development'. That would be a travesty of the facts. In essence, this division is still, like so many British companies, technology-led. The engineering function takes overall responsibility for idea generation and the marketing function approves or disapproves. It's the other way round than theory says it ought to be.

Or take the views expressed by the President of the wing of an American engineering firm:

Our industry is mature. It's not a 'go-go' industry. We're into cost-cutting. We are pretty product orientated around here. All of us spend a lot of time thinking about the product. One of the reasons is because we enjoy it. We like the product and we enjoy working with it.

It's not our intention to stay ahead of the pack. But we want to stay with them in terms of product features. But nearly all our design effort goes on cost reduction and commonality of components, so that we get economies of scale.

Using product change to react to competitive activity is a hit-and-miss approach to securing company survival, and one which is increasingly being challenged. The statement made by a development engineer in a division of the British chemical firm ICI is illustrative of the kind of transformations currently occurring:

Traditionally we have been technology-led. Recently, however, a new set of General Managers has been appointed to head up business areas. The appointments have gone to people who are businessmen first and chemists second. Their job is to drive their businesses forward. It's an enormous change in attitude and approach, particularly to product development. Initiatives are pursued now because they will make money, either in the short or in the long run. Previously, we did things because it was technically an excellent idea.

We believe that the above quotation provides insight into what is happening across more and more firms in all industry sectors. Because of a faster rate of market and product change, often forced upon domestic manufacturers by overseas competitors, increasing numbers of businesses are reorientating their whole approach to business and to product change. Such a reorientation alters the whole way in which a business considers the opportunities open to it. And, as we have seen, those businesses which have managed to become high achievers in product development pursue these efforts on the basis of a proactive strategy. It is proactive because it takes its lead from developments in the markets in which the business wants to compete. This requires vision on the part of top management and a willingness to take risks. In addition, it also requires top management to understand the full range of strategic choices which can be mobilized for product change.

The search for better strategic choices

Strategic choices in product development are critical. It is an important step for top management to accept the need to change its products so that these move forward with the needs of selected markets. It is done proactively by high achievers. When top management elects to pursue a proactive strategy, careful evaluation of potential strategic options is absolutely essential.

The range of strategic product development choices open to a business was reviewed in chapter 2. The purpose of the present section is to describe the strategic choices pursued by the high achievers, on the one hand, and the less successful product developer firms, on the other. In this respect one clear distinguishing feature of high achiever businesses is their willingness to engage actively in both product improvement and in new product development. All high achiever businesses in our sample did so, while only 50 per cent of the less successful businesses did so.

For the purpose of driving a business forward organically we would assert that both types of product development are important. Of special importance is the balance between product improvement and new product development. The issue was highlighted well by the managing director of a division of the British firm Bowater:

We've been highly successful on the basis of developing a completely new packaging product. But that was seven years ago. Of course we have improved the original product. But if we are going to sustain our rate of growth, we need to invest in new product development at appropriate stages. If we don't do this, we will go the way of many first generation businesses – we will have risen like a meteor and then dropped. What keeps me awake at night is how to keep going up.

The managing director's fears are well grounded. Many previously well-known firms have had to put up the shutters because their products no longer allowed them to compete satisfactorily. Sometimes such firms, after a long period of neglecting their existing product lines, have sought to rectify the situation by engaging in a crash program of new product development. This form of emergency action is dangerous because it simultaneously involves the highest risks, costs and also the longest likely pay-back. For example, the old British Austin–Rover motor manufacturing firm failed to develop its wide range of products adequately through their lives. Instead, the company pinned hopes on totally new models which appeared at ever-lengthening intervals. Many of Austin–Rover's competitors, on the other hand, invested in regular product improvement, as well as in new product development, and thereby achieved a more balanced offering in the marketplace. They also thus achieved a healthier combination of investment and risk.

There can be no doubt that product improvement is vital. Many Japanese firms are masters at product improvement by using a very wide range of options. But, at some stage, completely new product lines will be required by a business if it wants to grow. Unfortunately for many British businesses, the range of product development options open to them can be quite limited because of the relatively small size of British firms in world terms. This issue was highlighted in a British power tool manufacturing business:

In the league of companies we are relatively small. We are certainly in the second league, possibly in the third. Hence we have needed to specialize in particular types of power tools. We have chosen the industrial side, rather than the growing home-based side. We are, therefore, a specialist company – a nicher. But even in our specialist field we have big and aggressive competitors. . . .

You know, the whole range of power tools is concerned with making holes in everything from steel to concrete. We are fully aware that, one day in the future, laser technology will allow these functions to be performed differently. But we simply can't explore these technical possibilities because our small size will not allow us to fund the R&D costs involved.

This dilemma was stressed to us time and time again in British businesses. Bearing in mind that our investigation focused on businesses which were part of larger corporations, the problem would appear to stem from excessive hunger on the part of corporate parents for short-term profits. Unfortunately, many businesses allow themselves to be intimidated by headquarters' pressure for short-term results, and in consequence concentrate on safe incremental product developments. A British manufacturer of adhesive products spelled out the operational consequences as follows:

Safety first is the first axiom of our development work. That's why we suffer from an excessively narrow approach. Anything exciting and risky is done by acquisition.

Even in firms which have recently undergone a transformation, such as the British computer manufacturer ICL, there is constant pressure on the part of business managers for short-term profits. One manager lamented:

I am always being told: 'watch the bread and butter [existing products] –

don't just go for the jam' [new products]. It's irritating, particularly when I'm generating the income which will in time allow us to break out into new areas. I'm after a balanced portfolio of products for my business.

The difficulties highlighted above, which we believe are common across a broad sweep of British and American manufacturing, make urgent the need for wise choices concerning product development options. Product improvement is important to safeguard the existing customer base. Similarly, new product development is important to capitalize on longer-term growth opportunities.

The high costs and risks which commonly accompany new product developments are a major problem for many businesses. Because of this, there is a need to move forward in a considered way. This is why the search is now on for product development options which do not rely primarily on the application of expensive technology. In this respect we found that a small number of high achiever businesses are forging forward in a most interesting way. In a way that is not costing nearly as much money as traditional, technology-based, new product development.

The new approach

The new way involves looking at opportunities for product development through market applications and marketing strengths and opportunities. This changed approach is now found even in parts of very large corporations. Here is an example of the new approach and how it is being put into practice in a division of a major American corporation. The words are those of a senior development specialist:

We have completely altered the way we approach product development. Historically, we invented things and then we reflected on what the new compounds might be used for. What we have learned to do is to focus efforts so that developments move forward with market needs. It's an enormous step for this proud technological giant to have to accept that technology will not win all the battles for us now.

Now we will develop a certain technology only if it is likely to help us compete in markets we want to be in. We have learned not to fall in love with any particular technology. We learned that the hard way when a competitor hit us in a traditional market with a different technology. ... We thought we were operating in a mature market which we dominated.

After careful analysis we found that we dominated it because our major competitor had conceded the traditional part to us and moved on to open an expanding new part. This taught us the need to focus research into application areas. Now, 90 per cent of our research has this orientation; only 10 per cent is of the blue-sky type. Before it was nearly exactly the other way round.

This example demonstrates how important it is to conceptualize the market or markets in which a firm wants to compete. It entails moving away from a product-based understanding of the market to one which encompasses a way of combining the core dynamics of the marketplace with the company's core strengths. The top management approach adopted in a leading American food manufacturing corporation provides further insights:

We don't start with new product ideas. That's the old way. We start with a definition of opportunities. All the new products we are currently developing fell out of a study done on that basis. We started with an analysis of the needs, wants and aspirations of our customers. Then we looked to see how these might best be met using our existing strengths in marketing, distribution, manufacturing, etc. In this way we identified about 30 opportunities for new offerings, as I like to call them. We are now working on the top five.

Traditional new product development is often prohibitively expensive. We find that the new approach is far more cost effective because it's more focused. Further, because we can readily demonstrate that certain development options are necessary to safeguard the future of the whole business, we have a lot less resistance to our proposals. We do this by demonstrating that we are not seeking to enhance just our own sectional interests.

The new approach to product development was also in evidence in the American firm Black & Decker, where a senior manager stressed that they are now intent on exploiting all elements in the value chain for the purpose of enhancing product offerings. Hence, current product development strategy is increasingly based on capitalizing on the following strengths:

- Technology
- Manufacturing
- Marketing
- Sales
- Distribution
- After-sales service

In pursuing this analytical approach, Black & Decker aim to be leaders in interpreting emergent trends in markets in which they want to compete, and in understanding how core strengths can be manipulated to meet these trends. This is why (and how) their strategy is proactive, even though in execution they may on occasions be a 'fast second'.

The American food firm, Campbell, has taken the new approach to product development even further by encouraging the development of offerings aimed at meeting regional tastes. This has led the company to move towards dispersing manufacturing facilities. It has led to a reorganization of regional selling arrangements and to giving local marketing staff far greater say in new product development. Clearly, this is a strategy which will not automatically pay dividends in all fields. However, in food markets this decentralized approach is now being practised by companies like Pepsico's Frito-lay division and MacDonalds.

Organizational designs for product change

It hardly needs to be stressed that most companies today find themselves competing in circumstances of accelerating product change. When this is so (and this type of change afflicts all companies which we investigated) and no attempt is made to transform, the company will be overtaken by events.

The importance of organizational structure in a firm's ability to transform itself is well known. One of the first things that a firm does in a turn-around state is restructure. There are three practical questions tied up with the structure–change link; each concerns how organization structure can:

● stimulate radical change;
● stimulate incremental change;
● manage the existing business efficiently.

The problem is that each of these objectives is answered by a different form of organization structure. It is hardly surprising, therefore, that while acknowledging its vital importance, what constitutes an effective organizational design is still something of an enigma. What is clear, however, is a movement away from classic functional structures with many tiers of vertical management control and communication (figure 4.1). It is now widely recognized that undiluted functional specialization hinders change by preventing the lateral linkages required for effective interfunctional collaboration.

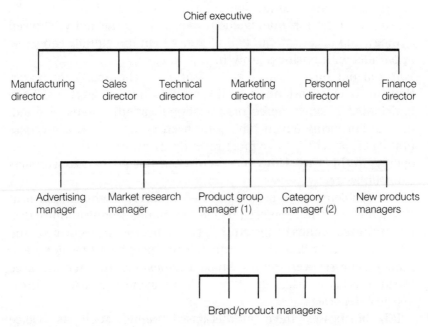

Figure 4.1:
The marketing arm of a wholly functionally based organization.

In wholly functionally based organizations, product development work is undertaken chiefly by marketing or technical specialists depending on which is the dominant function. The inherent multifunctional nature of product change is thus ignored by the organization structure, and it is left to individual managers to effect linkages as best they can.

Recognizing the severe limitations of wholly functionally based organizations, many firms are transforming themselves by restructuring on a business basis. In some companies this has been achieved through decentralization, and examples have already been given from firms on both sides of the Atlantic. The resulting more autonomous businesses then typically compete against each other for development funds. This is one of the most important organizational changes to have occurred in recent years as far as product development is concerned.

All other organizational innovations, such as 'innovation cells', or other special co-ordinating devices, are in our opinion secondary to changes made at the topmost level in a company. We make this assertion because business-based forms of organization provide the means whereby top management can achieve harmony between strategy and organization, and within which individuals can grow in parallel with business growth.

It will not have escaped the attention of the observant reader that, in focusing attention at the product market level, we have anticipated business-based organizational arrangements. We did, indeed, find firms which have long been organized on a business unit basis, or which have more recently transformed themselves to operate in this way. However, even when this is the case, conflicts can still occur.

The problems have been addressed squarely in the British firm ICL, which in 1983 replaced its old functional organization with a decentralized matrix structure. This change transformed the company so that it could operate in a business-based fashion. Separate businesses were set up, called 'business centres', within three broad market-focused divisions. ICL's business centres address 'usage categories'.

ICL businesses have market-based names such as 'Office Products', 'Retailing', or 'Local Government'. The sales and manufacturing functions are still centralized. The essential purpose of businesses is to focus on particular market opportunities and so give functional specialists a sense of belonging, particularly as far as product development efforts are concerned. The approach is based on exploiting market opportunities. It is quite different from the technology-push efforts of Advanced Technology Groups found in some high technology firms. The power of the business centre type of organization is in its freedom to choose how target markets are best served. In the words of a senior ICL manager:

The old ICL consisted of inflexible and loosely connected departments and geographic empires each organized along traditional functional lines. I knew exactly what to do strategically, but I hadn't got an organization to do it.

Each of the new Business Centres is now responsible for its own destiny. Centres are on average about 200 strong. Each is expected to have a formal organization chart, but at the same time everyone is clear that our efforts are not about those boxes on the chart. The game is now focused on attitudes and how good and flexible our attitudes are for capitalizing on business opportunities.

ICL's business-centre form of organization is mirrored in the major divisions of ICI which are now made up of several businesses, each headed by a Business General Manager whose job is to focus specialist inputs on selected market opportunities. As can be seen in figure 4.2 a typical ICI division still has functional heads for co-ordinating specialist inputs, such as marketing, manufacturing and technical, but the focus is now solidly on output maximization. As in many successful American firms, ICI has thereby introduced a leaner, though fitter, organization structure.

While the new organization has been criticized by some inside ICI for offering less positions for advancement, it does focus attention squarely on the bottom line. With only four tiers of management between the Principal Operating Officer and functional specialists, the contribution of all staff is now far more immediate and visible.

Creative organizational designs are vital for capturing both efficiency in managing the ongoing business and for generating the means by which new market opportunities can be comprehended and acted upon. But how do businesses handle specific projects for improving current products and developing new products?

Designs for managing product improvements

All the businesses in our sample actively undertake product improvement. Many less successful product developer firms had wholly functional structures in which, as has already been mentioned, product improvement activity tends to be located either with marketing or with technical line managers. In marketing-led businesses the initiative is normally taken by the product or brand managers themselves or by product planners. In technology-led businesses, product progression is normally the responsibility of the R&D Department. A lively R&D Department will do this proactively ahead of customers' requests; a less active department will do this reactively in response to requests or complaints.

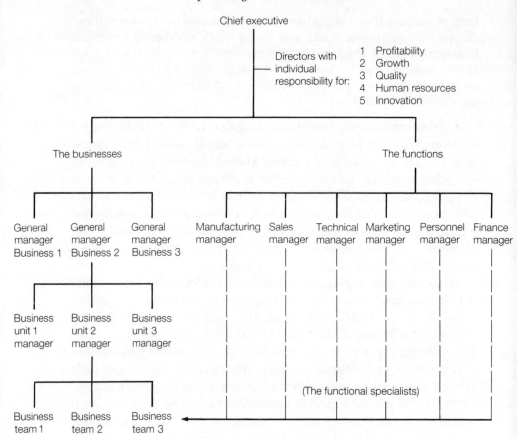

Figure 4.2:
A typical business-centred organization

When a business has literally hundreds of product updates under-way at any one time it may appoint a co-ordinator. We found this organizational arrangement popular when the technical function takes charge of developments. On its own, however, this organizational arrangement is insufficient to effect the needed co-operation with the marketing function.

Most of the high achievers in our sample made determined efforts to ensure linkages between their marketing and technical functions for the purpose of prioritizing product improvements. In functionally based firms, such linkages are effected by interdisciplinary teams of line managers operating in a matrix of responsibilities. In business-centred organizations, the interdisciplinary teamwork necessary emerged quite naturally.

Whenever such a multi-disciplinary team structure is in place, we observed that there is a far greater chance of autonomous product development. This type of development is not rigidly planned for, nor is it in response to customers' specific requests. It is the sort of development undertaken by individuals for a particular business. It is a manifestation of a team spirit fuelled by individual initiative.

In practice, there is a wide variety of team designs for managing product improvement and these are discussed in chapter 6. It is important to note here that the organizational mechanisms for product improvement used in high achieving firms display certain common characteristics: they encourage interdisciplinary co-operation, involve managers who are close to specific marketplaces, and promote market-led product improvement.

Designs for managing new product developments

Encouraging new product development in established businesses represents a major challenge. The main purpose is to encourage an existing business to rejuvenate itself. It is internal new business development. However, many businesses, even those which are becoming more adept at generating new products, are struggling to find the most appropriate organizational mechanisms.

We found that certain successful American product developer businesses are currently introducing what we regard as an interim organizational arrangement in firms which are still organized on a predominantly functional basis. It is a co-ordinating device found either in the marketing function or in the technical function or in both. Co-ordinators were given different names in different corporations. In a Black & Decker division the marketing function had appointed a Director New Products/New Markets, whose role was mirrored in the technical function by a Director of New Products. (The Director title in American firms signifies the first tier of management below that of Vice-President.) A similar organizational arrangement was in operation in the American white goods manufacturer Whirlpool, under the title Director R&D Marketing.

The job of these title holders is new product development for either existing markets or in new markets, using either existing technology or new technology. Fundamentally, their aim is to explore possibilities for exploiting all the product development options detailed in chapter 2. In operational terms, their job is that of change agent with the title of a very senior new product manager.

The contributions of Directors of New Products/New Markets is likely to be much affected by the messages concerning product development given out by top management. We make this assertion because time and time again it was stressed that reinforcement of shared values by top management may well have more influence on product development than formal organizational mechanisms. In the American firm Whirlpool, for example, top management reinforces the vision of its Director R&D Marketing by establishing 'innovation cells', their function being similar to what some analysts refer to as strategic planning units.[7]

In Whirlpool, innovation cells are headed by a marketing expert. The purpose of each cell is to capitalize on market opportunities. Anyone invited to serve in a cell is obliged to do so. This, in itself, is an important message to all concerned. It demonstrates that top management regards innovation as important. Innovation cells do not address solely product innovation opportunities, but all opportunities aimed at strengthening business operations through value chain examination. A similar arrangement was found in 3M in the form of Strategic Business Teams, which again are headed by persons with detailed knowledge of target markets.

In a number of high achiever businesses, we witnessed a determined effort to overcome deficiencies inherent in inducing new product development through organizational devices, such as new product managers. When this occurs the business is, in effect, turning its back on the philosophy popularized by writers such as Drucker who argued:

The search for innovation needs to be organized separately and outside the ongoing managerial business. Innovative organizations realize that one cannot simultaneously create the new and take care of what one already has ... taking care of tomorrow is far too big and difficult a task to be diluted with the concern for today.... Innovative organizations, therefore, put the new into separate organizational components concerned with the creation of the new.[8]

Interestingly, during our investigation we saw heavy emphasis in a number of corporations on autonomous, as opposed to induced, new product development. The terms 'induced' and 'autonomous' have been popularized by Robert Burgelman of Stanford University who has shown that some corporations now rely far less on large, purposively established, new venture departments for really new products.[9] Instead, they encourage business teams to emerge from within ongoing operations. It was stressed to us in a number of large corporations, both in Britain and America, that while ten years ago they had a new venture department with corporate responsibility for nurturing new products, their current approach is to encourage initiatives to grow out from established businesses.

The biggest potential advantage of the new approach is that the future of businesses is no longer inextricably linked with particular technologies, which in time will be overtaken by something newer. The new organizational approach is designed to encourage businesses to focus on changing markets as opportunities for further growth.

The new, autonomous, approach relies on identifying market requirements that can be exploited profitably by a business building on certain of its strengths. It is, in effect, new internal business development aimed at exploiting a new offering. What is novel about it is that the new product offering might not even involve using the existing manufacturing facilities. In the past, businesses have traditionally only considered new products for which they have manufacturing facilities. The new approach involves a far less restricted search for new products.

Operationally, the advantage of the new approach is that it need not be encumbered with heavy manufacturing overhead costs. Heavy costs are, however, loaded in at the front end – in identifying profitable opportunities. These front-end expenditures comprise primarily the costs of paying for gifted individuals who contribute to exploring new business propositions.

We saw increasing evidence that new product/new business development is now being pursued within divisions, rather than being imposed on them. This is important, but equally important is that within divisions, the pursuit of new products is handled differently from the pursuit of product improvements. Product or brand managers have the responsibility for improving existing products which utilize existing manufacturing facilities. But it is a set of different persons, from within a division that is looked to for developing really new products.

Some businesses have formalized the distinction by placing such persons into a separate department. Others have left the door open for individuals to take the initiative of their own accord, and provide these with freedom and resources to explore visions. In some companies this involves seeding visions in quite separate parts of the corporation, particularly if a business proposition conflicts excessively with that of ongoing operations.

Organizational problems

The organizational mechanisms used for new product development are discussed in detail in chapter 7. Of all the likely influences on product development success, organizational factors probably excite most passion. Not surprisingly it was in the less successful businesses that we were made acutely aware of the importance of this area of management. The problem confronting the head of the R&D function in a major American corporation with numerous self-standing businesses highlights the issues:

I have been in post two years. What I'm trying to do is to take the initiative as far as new product development is concerned. I am fighting a battle to convince the president that the marketing people need to take a stronger role in identifying new opportunities. His comment to me is: 'That's the job of your technical people'. He tells me that we have not been working on enough new products. But I personally don't think there is any point in going for numbers alone.

What we need are new products for which there is a good market. My department doesn't get that sort of market information. So I'm moving my technical people into the marketplace in a focused way – identifying and dealing with lead customers, for example. I know my people will be treading on toes, but our current marketing is solely selling to customers we've always done business with. I hope in time that the people I'm taking on will be able to merge into the businesses rather than staying under my control. Their job will be to focus on market opportunities and to feed information back on these.

I shall need to use the market information carefully, because heads of our businesses will react differently to suggestions about moving forward with new products. Some will continue to take a myopic view, others hopefully will be receptive to working with us in developing their product lines. So I'll pursue different approaches with different businesses.

The above comments reveal how huge, long-established American corporations can be afflicted by the most fundamental of organizational problems. Indeed, the contrast in corporations that have not restructured on a business basis with those that have are stark. This is so both in America and in Britain. We would venture the comment that such restructuring might not have been necessary had corporations pursuing a financial control style not insisted on systematically syphoning profits out of constituent businesses. It was this that has left many businesses in poor shape to face the more abrasive business climate of today.

Organizational problems also abound within operating businesses, and we found this to be so particularly in British firms. Indeed, in a high proportion of British firms there appears to be a reluctance to address organizational issues square-on. The comments made by the General Manager of a British paint manufacturing business illustrate the point:

Our organization chart is too complex, I know. What we do is to mould our organization chart around our people. I've got four sales managers reporting to me. I try to keep good people, so I organize around them. It does cause lots of problems. If you are going to run a muddled organization then it's important to have clear project management, which we've got.

Top management's essential task

Clearly, top management has a challenging task in determining an appropriate organization structure which allows both present and future competitive strengths to be exploited simultaneously. Indeed, in some of the most successful businesses, we witnessed a determined effort to achieve harmony between strategy and structure for this purpose. When successful in this respect, businesses become more human – they enter what some have referred to as 'the new era of activated enterprise'.[10] They provide excellent opportunities for employee participation; they promote a common value system; and they display a real commitment to the business they are in, rather than pursuing solely short-term financial goals.

Conclusion

It may appear self-evident, but the chief executive is the single most important person in an organization and certainly the most important influence on product development strategy and performance. The companies we talked to stressed repeatedly the word 'vision'. It is the responsibility of the chief executive of a business demonstrably to own and communicate a vision. Without this, the most talented marketing and technical managers will struggle. With it, the most hidebound and introspective business can begin to develop a market focus.

Our findings show that a market-focused product development vision will help a business overcome many of the hurdles that inhibit effective product development. It will certainly help to reduce the risks in product development by concentrating efforts in areas where the business stands the best chances of winning. It will keep creative persons interested and active in tailoring products to fit targeted markets. Most importantly, it will guard against being product or technology-led.

5

Using Teamwork to Complete Developments

WE turn now to the second set of factors which differentiate between high achievers and less successful product developers, namely those concerned with the actual readying of particular developments. While strategy determination and organizational choices are of great importance, the ultimate success of individual product developments depends on their successful execution. It is here that individual specialists can work together purposefully as a team, or waste time by pulling in different directions. In this chapter we explore what kind of teamwork is appropriate to specific development activities by contrasting the way teams work in high achieving and less successful product developer businesses.

Key product development activities

The improvement of an existing product or the development of a completely new manufactured product is not achieved instantaneously. In a manufacturing business, product development involves the following activities to a greater or lesser extent:

1 Product planning
2 Collection of ideas
3 Initial investigation
4 Initial screening
5 Priority analysis/assessment
6 Financial assessment/capital sanction
7 Physical development (including prototype)
8 Launch

However, in line with findings reported by other researchers who have investigated product development practices, we found that businesses rarely follow the above activities in strict sequence. This happens for a number of reasons. Some businesses have an undisciplined approach stemming from lack of experience. Others deliberately pursue certain activities in parallel in order to achieve speedy completion.

Undertaking product development activities in parallel rather than in sequence has been referred to as the 'rugby approach', where team members work together in parallel (as opposed to pursuing a 'relay approach'). Parallel development work is ideal for high value-added products where speedy development is critical for achieving profitability. In the relay approach individual functions typically take it in turns to attend to required tasks, meaning that development work will almost always take longer.[1]

Passing a project between functions in firms can undermine the ability to generate the cross-functional commitment and teamwork necessary for overcoming the inevitable obstacles and problems that will be encountered. On the other hand, while being faster, parallel development work will usually be more expensive, and is likely to be more difficult to control. However, these disadvantages are outweighed by the potential to respond to the marketplace faster.

The finding that firms rarely follow product development activities in strict sequential order led us to concentrate attention on certain key development activities. Regardless of their ordering, key activities do need to be performed, either implicitly or explicitly, in each and every product development. The names we gave these key activities are explained in table 5.1. They are:

A Planning product changes
B Idea exploration
C Screening and evaluation
D Physical development
E Launch

The focus of this chapter is on understanding how key activities are performed. And, in order to generate comparable results, a set of scales was developed to measure who is involved in each activity, and how work is controlled and co-ordinated.

Table 5.1   Key product development activities

Activities for which questions were asked	Key activities analysed	
1 Product planning	Planning product changes	(A)
2 Collection of ideas 3 Initial investigation	Idea exploration	(B)
4 Initial screening 5 Priority analysis/assessment 6 Financial assessment/capital sanction	Screening and evaluation	(C)
7 Physical development (including prototype stage)	Physical development	(D)
8 Launch (including formal test market)	Launch	(E)

Source: The five key activities used for analysing the findings are based on a schema developed by Crawford, C. M. (1983) *New Products Management.* Homewood, IL: Irwin p. 37.

Measurement scales

As was explained in chapter 3, understanding product development practice at the operating level concerns the 'soft' Ss of:

1 How **skills** are applied during each key development activity.
2 The input functions involved (**staff**).
3 The control and co-ordination of activities (**systems**).
4 The degree of top management hands-on control (**style**).
5 The number of levels of operating management participating in development work (**shared values**).

These five factors together form a mix of managerial variables which can be manipulated to generate the teamwork necessary to carry out effective product change. The scales used to measure these factors were based on those developed in earlier organizational research.[2]

The constructs underpinning each of the measurement scales are explained in box 5.1. During data collection a somewhat larger number of scales was used, as can be seen from the interview schedule in appendix 1. However, for the purpose of highlighting the most important operational differences between businesses, certain scores have been amalgamated. The criteria used for assessing product development practice for each separate activity (planning product changes through to launch) were:

1 **Skill**
2 **Staff specialization**
3 **Co-ordination** (to measure **systems**)
4 **Top control** (to measure **style**)
5 **Participation** (to measure **shared values**)

Because our investigation spanned a number of different industries in which development tasks vary in complexity, we made the scales as simple as possible so that these have general applicability. Each scale comprised a five point equal interval scale. In this way we measured **staff specialization** by assessing the number of different functions involved formally during each development activity. **Co-ordination** was a composite measure of the degree to which specific tasks are prescribed and carried out in a formal way. In other words, it is a measure of the degree to which procedures are systematized. **Top control** is a measure of the extent to which the head of the business exercises a style of management which relies on direct hands-on control of product development tasks.

Box 5.1   Criteria used to examine the management of key activities*

---

1 **Skills:** The degree of task specialization (TS-C) for undertaking specialized product development activities. In other words, the *'expertness'* with which each key activity is undertaken.

2 **Staff specialization:** The degree of division of labour achieved internally in terms of *functional participation* (TS-S).

3 **Co-ordination (systems):** The extent to which the activity is regularly monitored on a *formal* basis in meetings (FM) and the extent to which information concerning activities is passed in *writing* (FC).
   The degree to which roles have been defined in a *standard* way (ST) and how closely this *standard* way is normally adhered to (SC).

4 **Top control (style):** The extent to which the head of the business retains detailed *control* over the tasks involved (CC).

5 **Participation (shared values):** The *number of levels of management* formally involved in a hands-on way (CD).

---

* The capitals in brackets refer to the relevant question coding in the interview schedule (appendix 1). In the schedule analytical constructs were termed: **specialization; formalization; standardization; centralization; stratification** (configuration), as originally conceived by Pugh.[4] However, because of the high degree of correlation found between formalization and standardization, these two constructs were amalgamated for analysis purposes into one called 'co-ordination'. Stratification was renamed 'participation' to obtain insights into the extent to which top management facilitates the sharing of comon values.

We measured **skill** with reference to the 'expertness' with which each specific activity is undertaken. The degree of expertise (skill) was judged on the following criteria, derived from insights into successful practice that had been generated in previous research[3] into product development:

A **Planning product changes:** *skill* – the extent to which the product development program is an explicit part of the strategic planning process.

B **Idea exploration:** *skill* – the extent to which ideas are sought and tested against existing and likely future market opportunities rather than solely on an enhanced product feature basis.

C **Screening and evaluation:** *skill* – the extent to which common criteria but different hurdle rates are applied in assessing developments involving different degrees of risk.

D **Physical development:** *skill* – the extent to which both marketing and technical development work is undertaken in parallel during the physical development of the product.

E **Launch:** *skill* – the extent to which individual developments are rolled out in a carefully prepared and co-ordinated manner.

Participation is a measure of the number of levels of management involved formally in each of these tasks. As such it was used to provide an indirect measure of **shared values**: the extent to which commitment to a development project permeates the organization's managerial hierarchy.

Having explained the origins and development of the measurement scales used, we are now in a position to look at the managerial practices of the firms studied.

Teamwork practices

We turn first to specialized teamwork activities. The management of each activity from planning to launch is described by concentrating attention on the co-ordination and control of work. We shall deal with the five specialized product development activities in turn:

A Planning product changes
B Idea exploration
C Screening and evaluation
D Physical development
E Launch

Every firm was scored for each of the specialized development activities using the scales described earlier. For the purposes of exposition, we will draw on the experiences of all firms studied to provide insights into the managerial approaches necessary to implement product change. In this way the scores recorded both for high achievers and less successful product developers are reported. While these measures provide important insights into managerial approaches, the commentary (often using the words of the managers themselves) elaborates more fully the nature of actual practice. In addition, an indication is given in the tables of key differences between product improvement and new product development practices in high achiever firms.

A Planning product changes

High achiever businesses were much more *skilled*, on average, than less successful businesses in preparing themselves for product changes (table 5.2). The criterion used to assess this skill was 'the extent to which the product development program is an explicit part of the strategic planning process'. After all, both product improvements and new product developments alter a firm's approach to its opportunities and therefore affect its overall business goals and achievements. Without explicit recognition of product development activities in business planning mechanisms, product change will either not be undertaken at all, or will be pushed into areas unrelated to core operations or strengths.

We found that some firms, both in Britain and in America, have introduced highly sophisticated strategic planning procedures which require the formal integration of product development plans for each separate business. This happens particularly in *strategic planning* companies (like, for example, the British firms BOC, BP, Cadbury Schweppes, Lex, STC and United Biscuits). In these firms the corporate centre believes that it should participate in and influence the development of business unit strategies, often on the

Table 5.2 Scores for planning product changes (5 = high, 1 = low)

	High achiever businesses	Lower achiever businesses	Key differences
For product improvement	n = 20	n = 20	
Skill	3.6	1.7	+
Staff specialization	4.2	4.1	
Co-ordination	3.9	1.9	+
Top control	4.4	4.2	
Participation	4.8	3.9	+
For new product development	n = 20	n = 10*	
Skill	3.5	1.1	+
Staff specialization	3.7	3.8	
Co-ordination	2.1	2.8	+
Top control	4.3	4.2	
Participation	3.3	2.5	+

* Only ten of the lower achiever businesses had engaged in *new* product development in the last five years.

Source: Field study findings.

assumption that business unit managers can only be expected to look ahead into the short or medium term.

However, even in companies in which the corporate centre adopts a *strategic control* style in steering individual businesses on the basis of greater individual autonomy (firms such as Courtaulds, ICI, Plessey and Vickers in Britain) we found examples of very rigorous strategic planning procedures which integrate the product development plans of individual businesses. As far as American businesses are concerned, it must be stated that both the high achieving and the less successful firms in the sample, had a distinct preference for formal planning procedures.

Turning now to less successful businesses, we found, particularly in British firms, a widespread reliance on rudimentary product planning procedures based only on the need to prepare annual budgets. Not surprisingly, when this is the case, there is much less emphasis on integrating product development plans with corporate plans. This is the reason why less successful businesses score much lower on **skill**, on **co-ordination** and on **participation** for planning product improvements and also new product developments. The lower scores for participation in the less successful businesses reflect the effects of predominantly top-down planning. In many of these businesses any efforts at planning were focused solely on the very short term. Consider the following statements made by a senior manager in a British engineering firm:

We have product managers who are responsible for product amendments. The emphasis placed on updating, rationalizations and deletions depends on the corporate mood and on the current financial situation. We don't develop our new products in a conscious sort of way. Most new products are the result of lobbying done within the Executive Committee. New products have to be 'sold' to potential customers and also, very much, inside the company.

And similar sentiments expressed in another British firm:

We plan product developments one year ahead in line with the agreed budgets. Anything beyond that is a vision which is discussed with the chairman. We don't do much product planning. It's easier to bolster up old product lines – it's less hassle, and involves less begging for additional funds from the corporate centre. Also it's quicker to do product improvements – safer and more comfortable.

The dangers of not undertaking formal product planning are expressed well by the Marketing Director of a British manufacturer of adhesives:

We have tended to make decisions here on a day-to-day basis through fairly informal committees. One of the problems that arises is that both technical and commercial people work on several projects at the same time and there are always conflicts over resources. Our problem is that these conflicts don't get brought up and resolved formally at an early enough stage. So you end up with two or more projects both of which fail to be completed because they are constantly competing against each other for resources.

We would assert that, while product planning is important in all businesses, it is of especial importance in those that traditionally have relied on customers for new product initiatives. Such customer-active product innovation is common in machine tool manufacturing and in other businesses that have grown up to support large and powerful original equipment manufacturers. In these circumstances there is the constant danger that the business will react solely to customer initiatives. The issue was explained to us well in the American firm Cincinnati Milacron:

When you've got a finite number of engineers who can do new product development work, the danger is that these get sucked-in for repair and service work for existing customers. Only planning can guard against imbalances.

Engineering businesses, especially, are in constant danger of undertaking developments on an unplanned basis. For this reason some have had planning procedures imposed by the corporate centre. It was stressed to us that divisional or business managers often lack the skills necessary to formulate appropriate product development plans and in consequence it may be necessary to offer assistance.

Some corporations ensure that each division has a planner for this purpose. It is his or her responsibility to ensure that both a long-term and a shorter-term view is taken. The following slightly amended statement by a planner in an American corporation illustrates the procedure:

For each of our major market segments we developed a grid showing how large each was expected to be in the year 2000. We made assumptions about which other firms are likely to be competing in each of these markets. Then we built in an assessment of our present and future capabilities as suppliers.

From this analysis we concluded that we needed to (i) invest in certain new technologies, and (ii) identify new growth markets if we wanted to compete proactively. We decided, in conjunction with the divisional staff, to move businesses into a number of markets in which we had not been active players before. The product developments being undertaken now are based on this analysis.

It would be quite incorrect to give the impression that all high achieving businesses in our sample were parts of corporations which engage in strategic planning. Several successful businesses, particularly in Britain, were parts of corporations which still operate in a traditional planning mode in which past performance is projected forward without detailed analysis of likely competitive reactions or changes in specific market segments. It is difficult to predict how sustainable such an approach will be in the long term. Success in these circumstances may be due more to luck, market dominance or sleepy competition, than to any specific approach to 'planning' product change.

Mindful of the advantages to be gained from a market-led approach to planning product developments, the American firm 3M has established Strategic Planning Teams within individual divisions. These teams report directly to the General Manager of a division. The General Manager is responsible for co-ordinating their efforts in relation to needed resources. Progress is reviewed quarterly in depth – usually over several days – with all members of a team being required to attend. The purpose of these quarterly planning meetings is to prioritize ideas for the purpose of making best use of scarce development resources.

We see in 3M how top management adopts a **style** of managing which allows it to be directly involved in product development planning on a regular basis. Not unexpectedly, the degree of direct intervention is highest in the case of expensive new product developments. Yet at the same time there is wide participation in all product development decision making at regular periodic meetings to reinforce **shared values**.

It was stressed to us that 3M's Strategic Planning Teams, as is typical in innovative companies, have no problem in identifying opportunities for possible new products. But problems inevitably occur over prioritizing ideas and it is here that the planning mechanisms provide appropriate guidance. The underlying logic is to prioritize product opportunities in relation to market potentials – that is why each Strategic Business Team is headed up by a market specialist. Before the introduction of strategic business teams, most 3M divisions relied upon product managers pushing forward their individual product lines. The new approach focuses on market-based business opportunities, which allows far wider scope for product development.

It was in a large American food manufacturer that a clear distinction was evident between the strategic approach to product improvement compared with the approach adopted for new product development. As is typical in food companies, product improvements are the responsibility of brand managers reporting to a category manager. Nominally these managers also have responsibility for new product developments. But 'real' new product development (as it was put to us) is undertaken in a separate part of the organization under a vice-president responsible for strategy and development.

A member of the corporation's Strategy and Development department summarized the approach to planning new product development as follows:

We do not plan for *new* products in the same way as we do for improvements to our existing products. We don't start with new product ideas as such. We certainly don't think in terms of product line progression. What we do is to try to define a market opportunity. The product will fall out of this opportunity. Of course you can't look at all opportunities. We select in relation to our strengths. Any planning extends only so far as we know that we want to grow the division within those constraints.

In high achieving businesses, plans for product change were both developed and monitored through some form of regular (usually monthly) product policy meeting. This forum provides the setting for generating the right kind of managerial momentum for product change. Adjustments to plans can be widely considered and agreed to, and resource conflicts addressed head-on. In less successful businesses, both in America and in Britain, we often found that these meetings were either not held on a regular basis, or that top management failed to attend them regularly. When this happens top management risks sending a 'hidden message' which indicates that product development is not seen as being as important as the running of the existing business.

We also found in high achiever businesses that, in the case of planning new product developments, there is markedly less co-ordination in the form of written guidance or procedures. This is not really surprising, because while the need for new products might be identified in the planning process, there are no tried and tested procedures for envisioning the precise form such new products might ultimately take. The score for participation was found to be much lower for new product planning, too, which reflects a common reluctance on the part of top management to involve a wide spread of personnel in what is a most sensitive area in commercial operations.

Fewer staff specialists (in terms of functions) were found to be involved in new product development in high achieving firms than for product improvement. This is because new product developments are frequently left to the initiative of those marketing and technical specialists who are acknowledged as being the most capable of envisioning new business opportunities. In the case of product improvements, a wider set of functions is regularly involved.

B Idea Exploration

The scores for exploring ideas for product improvements mask important differences in approach between high achieving and less successful product developer firms (table 5.3). While both sets of businesses are able to report that a wide number of idea sources and staff are drawn upon in this activity, it is the way these factors are mobilized and utilized which is the key to understanding the approaches adopted.

Table 5.3 Scores for idea exploration (5 = high, 1 = low)

	High achiever businesses	Lower achiever businesses	Key differences
For product improvement	*n* = 20	*n* = 20	
Skill	3.6	3.3	
Staff specialization	4.3	3.8	
Co-ordination	4.2	3.9	
Top control	2.2	2.6	
Participation	3.9	3.7	
For new product development	*n* = 20	*n* = 10*	
Skill	4.3	2.8	+
Staff specialization	2.3	3.3	+
Co-ordination	3.1	4.2	+
Top control	2.9	4.0	+
Participation	3.4	2.8	+

* Only ten of the lower achiever businesses had engaged in *new* product development in the last five years.

Source: Field study findings.

Particularly, the **skill** scores for product improvement and also for new product development mask important differences. In successful businesses the generation of ideas frequently occurs spontaneously and does not require artificial stimulation through brainstorming or similar techniques. This was stressed to us forcefully by a marketing manager at 3M in the following words:

There's no problem with shortages for new product ideas. The problem is screening out, so that you explore the right ideas. In this respect we've now trained ourselves to ask: 'What's the size of the nut?' That is to say, what potential business can result? Not just whether it is technically new and exciting.

The situation in less successful product developer businesses was often quite different, as was explained by a development engineer in a British mechanical engineering firm:

In our business we have never been awash with ideas for possible new products. Perhaps that has been because we have not had appropriate forums for these to emerge and to pursue them in concept. Consequently, most of the ideas are suggested by senior management, and then are taken up by lower management with varying degrees of enthusiasm.

It is in collecting and exploring ideas for new products that particularly sharp distinctions arise between high achieving and less successful businesses, as can be seen from table 5.3. We found that a number of successful businesses, particularly in America, have adopted a similar schema to that used in Procter & Gamble for flagging-up ideas for possible new products. This involves sending senior management a short (often two page) document entitled 'Basis for Interest' in which an opportunity is outlined and funds are requested to explore it further in concept.

We found that many successful businesses make determined efforts to focus on the business opportunity ('the size of the nut') at the idea exploration stage, rather than on product features, particularly in the case of ideas for new products. The philosophy was explained to us in a 3M division as follows:

Previously we had product managers pushing to extend their product lines. We now regard this as an outmoded way to pursue new product developments. You don't want emphasis on product features overriding emphasis on market opportunities. The lead for future products must come from the market – not solely from product champions. So, with us now, ideas for possible new products are steered by the division's market managers and not the product managers.

It is important to emphasize that the above respondent was talking about exploring ideas for internal or organic new product development. He was not concerned with what in some businesses is referred to as new venture management. All the new products being explored were related in some way to the company's existing business strengths. What is different about the approach is that it is grounded in interpreting market needs rather than merely on exploring the feasibility of improving this or that product feature. As such, it is quite different from business development through 'big-bang' product innovation, amalgamation or unrelated diversification, which are the typical stock in trade of New Venture Divisions.

In the American white goods manufacturer Whirlpool we also found evidence of the new approach. A senior manager explained:

I want to reverse the traditional way for developing *new* products. Traditionally, the way we distribute, sell, etc. have all been treated as constraints into which each new product development must fit. My approach is different. I look at new product development on the basis of the market opportunity it offers rather than on the basis of the technical opportunity. So I say to my people 'let's start with a customer focus, not a product or technology focus and then let's set about providing the highest added value new product'.

A remarkably similar approach was in evidence in the British earth-moving equipment firm JCB, where a technical director remarked:

While our new products are still basically engineering-led we do make a determined effort to approach the challenge of exploring ideas from the point of view of the business opportunity. Of course, you can't quantify everything exactly, but it's important to get to grips as far as you can with the likely potential. We do our best estimates before investing any sizeable amounts of money.

The above statement raises the important question of how far it is possible at the idea exploration stage to quantify the likely market potential for an envisaged new product. In several businesses this task was placed at the feet of the marketing function. But, at the same time, many of our technical respondents expressed disappointment, if not frustration, with their marketing counterparts who were widely accused of being reluctant to quantify market potentials. The following lament captures the spirit of these complaints:

I find marketing people rather disappointing in terms of thinking up completely new product concepts. They have an unfortunate tendency to say, because there is not already an established direct competitor for a possible new product, there is unlikely to be a market for it.

But marketing input is absolutely essential 'up-front'. It's far better to lose £50,000 up-front and learn from the experience than to lose £1,500,000 and get demoralized when you have to stop half way through development.... It's absolutely shattering for the technical people, several of whom may have been coming in until midnight for weeks to work on a project.

Despite the importance of accurate marketing input at the idea exploration stage we identified very few businesses in which such marketing effort is directly charged against specific projects, as is standard practice for technical activities. This is because marketing effort, far more widely than technical effort, is still predominantly costed as an overhead. In this connection, several technical respondents argued in favour of higher degrees of **co-ordination** in the case of marketing input for exploring ideas. A chief design engineer in a British firm commented:

I would like to see a more formalized system for exploring ideas. We in engineering have always needed to put things down on paper because we are spending money. But this sort of discipline is missing on the marketing and sales side. Really, the technical function could benefit enormously from some systematic, properly documented, marketing input right from the start of the product development process. ... But it's very difficult to get marketing people to commit themselves in this way. It's criminal if they don't, because if things go wrong they can push the blame on others. I'm here ten hours a day and can't go out to potential customers. I need marketing input ... not just sales projections.

So, in the case of both product improvement and new product development, it is the way idea exploration is carried out and directed which discriminates between our sample firms. The scoring differences in idea exploration for new product development rest largely with the pragmatic approach adopted by less successful product developers. Less successful businesses are commonly heavily locked into their existing product base. In these firms top management feels an obligation to initiate the exploration of new product ideas (resulting in high top control scores and low participation scores).

What successful businesses appear to have learned is to loosen themselves up for the purpose of exploring new product concepts and for the purpose of facilitating choices. Some of the successful businesses visited have been highly successful in achieving this. In many cases their novel approach to really new product development has been forced on them by threats to their existing business. However, irrespective of the cause, the new approach to exploring new product ideas engenders a more adventuresome, less traditional and less incremental exploration of possibilities.

However, the new approach now being practised in exploring new product ideas is not universally popular inside firms, as was explained by an American food manufacturer:

There are many traditionalists in the company who would like to get us under control. But everything which we are attempting has been open to them as an opportunity before. Having said that, I must say that the resistance to our efforts is not great, mainly because our exploration is low cost compared with product developments in the established areas.

Despite having provided examples from American firms, we did find evidence in a number of successful British product innovator businesses of acceptance of the new approach, as is illustrated by a senior business centre manager in ICL:

We are attempting to encourage our young people to take business risks by asking for money for exploring new product ideas. If things go wrong they know that they will not suffer if the situation rather than the analysis was to blame.

The approach in less successful product developer businesses was often starkly different, as can be seen from the following statement by the Director, Advanced Engineering, in an American food processing manufacturing firm:

No, monies would not be asked for by bright individuals, as you put it, to spend for exploratory purposes. We do not have that sort of entrepreneurial approach in this company.

An important difference observed was in the **skills** applied for handling concepts for product improvement as opposed to new product concepts in successful businesses. Product improvement concepts are typically generated with the aim of enhancing existing features. Work tends to involve a wide range of functional specialists at many levels within the company. In contrast, new product ideas are increasingly being generated against envisioned market opportunities. And, as in the case of planning, significantly less functional specialists may be involved in exploring these ideas in concept.

In the most lively product innovator businesses we came across impressive examples of the marketing and technical functions working together very closely. It was often emphasized to us that idea exploration is a most important task in successful businesses because these are often brimming over with suggestions for product changes from lively and well-motivated staff.

C Screening and evaluation

As far as **skills** in screening are concerned, we found that high achiever businesses are far more likely to apply common criteria to assessing product development proposals than are less successful businesses. However, few businesses appear to make a systematic attempt at applying different hurdle rates for propositions involving different degrees of risk. There were, of course, exceptions, particularly among high achiever firms. A senior manager in an American business remarked:

I get nervous about the word entrepreneur because that implies risk-taking. I don't want people who are crazy risk-takers. What I want are persons who are extremely good at risk assessment, which I consider is very different.

Undertaking accurate screening of ongoing work is important, but so is speed in coming to decisions. In many less successful businesses, managers often lamented the time taken by their executive committees to reach screening decisions. This complaint was widely voiced in British companies. The technical director of a British engineering firm (classified as less successful in the sample) explained:

Contact with competitors suggests that it takes us no longer than them to do physical product development. But they beat us because they are quicker during the decision-making process. It seems to me that their disciplines in progressing developments allow them to be faster. This includes particularly the initial decision on whether or not to go ahead with a particular development.

The similarity in the **co-ordination** scores for both sets of businesses masks a fundamental difference. In high achiever businesses, screening and evaluation is maintained as an ongoing activity throughout the development process. In the case of less successful businesses, screening tended to be an activity occurring formally only once in the early stages of the development. As such, it is a snapshot approach to understanding the value of a development; a snapshot taken at a point at which information is particularly vague. Consider the statement made by an American earth-moving equipment manufacturing business:

Once we get something in iron – by that I mean build a prototype – it goes on and on. I have been involved in programs which date back to 1969! At that time I personally felt we should not be spending money on them. On one we spent over $4,000,000. But we never went into production, because the function is now performed in quite a different way.

In all businesses we came across great reluctance to stop developments. This is understandable because of the demotivating influence of stopping a development in its tracks. However, in a considerable number of less successful product developers, both in Britain and in America, it was obvious that there were slack systems in place for screening and evaluation. This meant that once started, product updates, as well as new product developments, trundled on. Pet projects which had the support of top management received priority in terms of resources; other projects had to take their turn.

The situation was different in the majority of high achiever businesses. At best, monthly assessment reviews under the direct control of the chief executive checked program progress. Strategic reviews might then take place quarterly or twice yearly. The purpose of the monthly assessment reviews was to release the resources needed for particular projects. It was common for the heads of participating functions to have to append their signatures to specific development programs, which serves as formal acknowledgement to provide support at the scheduled times. And, as can be seen from table 5.4, a much wider range of staff functions was involved than in less successful businesses.

Not surprisingly, in the high achiever businesses we found top control to be far more pronounced during screening and evaluation than in the less successful businesses. In fact, this was an important distinguishing characteristic of these types of businesses: the head assumed responsibility for the ultimate success of product developments. Such control, however, was not exercised unilaterally. Screening and evaluation considerations were openly discussed with all participants in strategic reviews. This joint decision making is reflected in much higher **participation** scores (table 5.4).

The situation in less successful product developer businesses was typified by less co-ordinated teamwork. It is illustrated in the fol-

Table 5.4 Scores for screening and evaluation (5 = high, 1 = low)

	High achiever businesses	Lower achiever businesses	Key differences
For product improvement	*n* = 20	*n* = 20	
Skill	3.4	2.6	+
Staff specialization	3.5	3.0	
Co-ordination	4.4	4.2	
Top control	4.5	3.4	+
Participation	4.3	3.7	+
For new product development	*n* = 20	*n* = 10*	
Skill	4.2	2.9	+
Staff specialization	3.4	2.8	+
Co-ordination	4.3	4.2	
Top control	4.5	3.5	+
Participation	4.2	2.9	+

* Only ten of the lower achiever businesses had engaged in *new* product development in the last five years.

Source: Field study findings.

lowing comments made by the new product manager in a British electrical engineering firm:

As new product manager I take along to the heads of functions ideas I've got or have received – sometimes from outsiders – to see what they think. They do the initial screening. If any of them does not like the idea it's the end of the matter. If they raise no objections, I will subsequently raise it in a somewhat more developed state at the new products committee meeting. After that we might decide to pass it on to the executive board for final approval.

The above comments illustrate the ways in which top management can involve itself in screening and evaluation. Top management can either avoid being directly associated with any particular project, or it can indicate clearly to others that it regards product development progress as important. At worst, top management will use indirect methods for screening and will sanction only safe, relatively low risk developments. While this approach can protect top management's job in the short run, it is likely to jeopardize the long-run future of a business.

An important difference observed in high achiever firms between product improvement and new product development during 'up-front' activities was in the **skill** applied for screening and evaluation. Some successful businesses distinguish themselves by applying different hurdle rates for assessing new product developments which involve different degrees of risk. Such hurdle rates emphasize the value of assessing the long-term strategic business opportunity of a new product concept, rather than merely reflecting the routine application of pay-back measures. Simple pay-back measures are far more appropriate for screening and evaluating product improvement proposals, as opposed to proposals for completely new products.

Essentially, the task of screening and evaluation is to check on an ongoing basis that developments being pursued are in accord with top management's vision for the future of the business. This task cannot be delegated. We believe that it can be achieved satisfactorily only when clear objectives and criteria are established which are explained to managers at different levels. In this way top, middle and lower level managers can be encouraged to involve themselves as a team in ensuring that sound judgements are made in respect of product changes designed to protect the future of the business.

D Physical development

We turn now to what is popularly regarded as the essence of product development, namely the physical readying of the intended offering. Far from being a discrete stand-alone activity, we shall see that what is involved is the culmination of decisions taken during the important up-front activities already considered. In this section we shall show that high achieving businesses approach the task of physical development quite differently from less successful product developers. The key differences are in the way in which separate specialists work together to ready the intended product, so that it is completed as quickly as possible and meets business objectives.

Physical development most clearly differentiates approaches to product development in the two groups of firms for both product improvement and for new product development (table 5.5). **Skill** scores are lower for less successful firms because so many of these have yet to adopt an interfunctional project team approach. Interfunctional project teamwork involves more than having representatives from different functions, as is implied in matrix forms of organization. It involves different functions working together and continually interacting during physical development of a product.

Table 5.5 Scores for physical development (5 = high, 1 = low)

	High achiever businesses	Lower achiever businesses	Key differences
For product improvement	*n* = 20	*n* = 20	
Skill	4.2	2.9	+
Staff specialization	4.7	4.4	
Co-ordination	4.6	3.2	+
Top control	2.7	2.8	
Participation	4.7	3.4	+
For new product development	*n* = 20	*n* = 10*	
Skill	4.4	2.6	+
Staff specialization	3.8	3.9	
Co-ordination	3.3	4.6	+
Top control	3.8	2.7	+
Participation	4.6	3.4	+

* Only ten of the lower achiever businesses had engaged in *new* product development in the last five years.

Source: Field study findings.

In essence, the managerial objective of the physical development phase is to overcome the problems highlighted in the following comments made by a chief development engineer in an American firm:

The real snags come from marketing. When they see the developed product it's often not what they expected or wanted. That's why I believe more of the initiative for developments should come from marketing. Recently, for example, top management stipulated a cost-reduction program. That inevitably affected the look of the finished product. When marketing saw the outcome, they said it looked cheap and that they could not sell it. So the specs had to be changed yet again. It would be helpful if marketing told us what they wanted earlier ... not after we've done the work.

Not only do these comments highlight inadequacies in the marketing remit, they also point to the fact that physical development is often perceived by participants to be 'the technical function's job'.

In high achiever businesses great emphasis was placed on communication between different specialists involved in physical development work. Many businesses set aside meeting rooms for stimulating informal teamwork. This is a very necessary facility, because in successful product innovator businesses, brand managers typically call a great number of meetings for the purpose of exploring possibilities. Other specialists will attend these meetings if they see some point in contributing, hence a meeting room on neutral territory is often preferred. Indeed, in some businesses important meetings are conducted in the simulated competitive environment of a 'War Room', in which progress on important projects is charted around the walls.

In almost all businesses visited, and certainly in all the high achievers, there is now great emphasis on completing developments as quickly as possible. The common aim is to halve development times, but often the aim is to do even better than that. To encourage more effective teamwork we found that a number of successful businesses place great emphasis on teamwork. A common saying in these businesses is: 'Development is too important to be left to brilliant individuals'. What is being emphasized is that development cannot be left to functional specialists working solely for perfection within their function. What is needed is to aim for business success.

Important differences were observed in the way high achievers and less successful businesses **co-ordinate** their physical development efforts. This is an important issue, because our evidence points to the advantage of using different types of procedures for product improvement, as opposed to new product developments. In undertaking product improvement, successful businesses prefer rigorous co-ordination in order to check that what was intended to be developed is in fact being executed according to the agreed timetable. It will be remembered that the heads of the different participating functions may, in fact, have signed their agreement to provide resources.

In almost all of the high achieving businesses, and in all the successful American businesses, there existed a product development guide or manual of some sort. However, in many businesses it was stressed that while developments follow the spirit indicated in the manual, in practice it is often necessary to deviate. Nevertheless, in all cases, respondents considered it important to have regular checks on progress and to reconcile claims for scarce development resources. At their most basic such checks involve 'signing-off' at particular stages in the development process.

For new product development we found the situation quite different. In businesses practising the new approach, the emphasis is on developing the entire business concept, not just the product hardware. In a division of DuPont which has established a 'hatchery' for new products the situation was described as follows:

Each team in the hatchery is headed by an entrepreneurial leader. It's his responsibility to literally create a new business based on making available a superior offering for the part of the market being aimed for. For this purpose we give him the mandate to make deals with potential partners and customers. He has the authority to create a whole new business. His team is multi-functional. He can have persons on his team from outside the company.

We have found the concept of teams useful in situations of technical complexity and high uncertainty. Teams find ways to solve things quickly. They have to. If they don't, there is no reason for them existing. It used to take 10–20 years to come up with something really new. Our new approach has cut this down to a few years.

And again in Kraft, it was stressed that a lot of latitude is deliberately given in the development process for really new products. A senior manager described his job as follows:

I don't automatically think of making a new product in our existing plant. We may, in fact, not even use our own R&D facilities. This would be unthinkable in ordinary line management. When I was a category manager on the cheese side, I had to stick to the product development rules. Now I'm learning to break some of those rules in the interests of achieving speedy new product development. If I don't, the competition will beat us to it.

It's costly because I move forward on parallel tracks – not sequentially. It's risky. I'm saying to top management: 'If all goes well, we shall need $5,000,000 next year; if it doesn't, we'll pull out and lose less.' But they expect me to quantify the risk pretty accurately.

The situation in less successful businesses was different with regard to **co-ordination**. It was less a matter of not having a system to co-ordinate product improvements, as one of how to use the system efficiently. In many businesses the dangers of top management meddling were lamented, because this slows down development times and means that decisions are taken on an apparently irrational basis. Worse still, top management interference can result in a lack of a sense of ownership on the part of those charged with day-to-day tasks. Not infrequently, this encouraged functional specialists to seek satisfaction within sectional professional interests, rather than in the business success of projects.

At worst, for product improvement, we found that decisions were taken on a purely verbal basis and then written up afterwards to provide justification for a particular course of action. When this occurred there was, typically, no 'living product development document' with which specialist contributors could associate closely. The following statement made by a development engineer in a British business illustrates the weaknesses of this method:

We monitor product development progress by exception. We don't even discuss a program formally if its going OK. True, we do have a project co-ordinator, but his job is to check and record progress solely within Engineering.

The use of a project co-ordinator or program manager was common *within* the technical function in the less successful businesses. What distinguishes successful businesses is that the co-ordination is undertaken *across* functions. A development manual, however rudimentary, which requires individual functional specialists to sign off their contributions, can help greatly in achieving such co-ordination.

Of great importance are differences in the direct involvement or **control** by top management. In high achieving product developers, top management provides support for both product improvements and new product developments by active involvement. In the case of product improvements, support is indirect; in the case of new product developments, it is far more hands-on. It will be remembered that top management support is likely to have been in evidence during idea generation and exploration when sums of money were made available for exploratory purposes. During physical development, top management support and interest translates into active participation in the case of important new product developments. However, development work on strategically less important product improvements is frequently left to those most intimately involved.

We found the situation quite different in most less successful product developer firms. In these, top management is frequently grudging in its support of product development initiatives. At worst, particularly in the case of new product developments, top management will distance itself from development work until it becomes clear that success is assured. Top management therefore rarely gets involved directly in either product improvements or new product developments.

With regard to **participation** we found key differences between high achievers and less successful businesses. The successful businesses formally involve a wider spread of management than the less successful ones. This is a reflection both of the greater measure of teamwork apparent in these firms and also of the importance of product development work in the company as a whole.

During development, important differences between managing product improvements and new product developments were again observed in successful firms (table 5.5). The number of different staff specialists involved was much lower for new product developments because it is a small closely knit team which puts together propositions of strategic importance. This form of new product/new business development is discussed in chapter 7. It also accounts for the lower co-ordination scores. Not surprisingly, control by top management is markedly higher in the case of new products for both physical development and for launch: the head of the business rightly takes detailed interest in both of these activities, because, in the case of important new products, failures at either stage can threaten the existence of the whole business. These tasks are, therefore, less likely to be delegated on a routine basis, as is typically the case with product improvements.

E Launch

The scores recorded for managing the launch phase are remarkably similar (table 5.6). Such a picture is not surprising. All businesses take this final activity seriously. For high achieving firms, the launch represents the crowning glory of all the hard work undertaken so far. Such firms are acutely aware that a mismanaged launch can ruin a new development's chances, even if the product itself is sound and has been thoroughly tested. For these reasons, the launch of both product improvements and new product developments feature tight co-ordination and widespread interfunctional team and line management involvement.

These managerial practices are also apparent in less successful product developer firms – but are often motivated by very different reasons. A product has been developed (quite often primarily by technical specialists) for which the marketing and sales functions now need to find an appropriate market. Tighter co-ordination and wider participation in the launch phase may, however, represent in these firms a frantic attempt to get the product 'off the workbench' and into the market. Often this is driven by top management which

Table 5.6 Scores for launch (5 = high, 1 = low)

	High achiever businesses	Lower achiever businesses	Key differences
For product improvement	n = 20	n = 20	
Skill	4.3	4.1	
Staff specialization	4.6	4.4	
Co-ordination	4.4	3.8	+
Top control	2.8	2.9	
Participation	4.6	4.4	
For new product development	n = 20	n = 10*	
Skill	4.6	4.0	+
Staff specialization	4.7	4.3	
Co-ordination	4.6	3.6	+
Top control	4.6	4.2	
Participation	4.5	4.2	

* Only ten of the lower achiever businesses had engaged in *new* product development in the last five years.

Source: Field study findings.

has become aware of the development rather late and now stipulates launch parameters to minimize the chances of failure. Sometimes a product launch becomes a tactic used in an attempt to thwart competitive activity. For whatever reason, it is apparent that the launch in many of the less successful firms is an end in itself, rather than the culmination of a carefully worked through product development process.

Given the apparent similarity of the managerial practices in high achiever firms and in the less successful product developers, commentary on certain closely related launch issues to which respondents drew attention is helpful.

In several high achieving businesses, an internal publication entitled something like 'Global New Product Introduction System' has been issued to staff, or is now being prepared. This is intended to guide developments in such a way that these are undertaken with constant reference to selected market opportunities. The guide is not intended to detract from creativity in the development process, its purpose is as an *aide-mémoire*. Reference to it throughout all development activities is intended to ensure that when the new product is launched there is not a wild scramble to find a market here and a market there.

The issue was highlighted by a senior manager in a British electronics firm:

We probably develop better products than the Americans but we don't exploit them as well. My personal belief is that this is because we spend less 'up-front' on marketing in particular. I spend about 2 per cent of turnover on market research related activities and I suspect many of our American competitors spend a lot more.

Product development has traditionally been marketing-led in food manufacturing firms. In these firms much emphasis has in the past been placed on test marketing techniques to assess customers' reactions. However, many food manufacturers stressed that this can involve lengthy delays and other problems. The issues are highlighted by an American food manufacturer:

We are using computer market share prediction models much more than we used to. Test marketing is virtually impossible these days because when you've gone public with an idea it may be a year before you are ready to go into the marketplace. Remember, it takes us a minimum of six months to one year to read a test market accurately. Meanwhile the competition knows exactly what we are up to. They then try to destroy the test by dropping coupons, running extra ads, etc.

Many established American food manufacturing businesses stressed the importance of speed in launching products. A frequent complaint was that they were slower to launch new products than new entrants who had no national reputation to dent in the event of a new product failure. The fear of product launch failure was also frequently mentioned in British food manufacturing firms.

Clearly it is a matter of philosophy or strategy whether a business is prepared to risk a product failure or not. In the electronics industry, it is common practice to launch new models before all the technical bugs are ironed out. In the electronics market, certain customers are normally eagerly waiting for products with enhanced features for which they are prepared to pay a premium price, hence it is important to hit the market early with new products. However, the wisdom of a fast development policy is difficult to assess accurately and is highly dependent on supplier–customer relationships and the quickness of the manufacturer's response to technical problems.

We gained the impression that management in less successful product developers is far more reluctant to countenance a product launch failure. For this reason, top management can suddenly become actively involved in the latter parts of the development process, after having remained aloof from earlier activities. This can mean that products are launched with inadequate preparation, or ironically, that the launch process is delayed while top management is consulted (or introduces new issues in the launch process). In these companies there is often a wish to reduce the risk of product launch failure to near zero. Not only is this an unobtainable goal (and for this reason will inhibit product change of any kind), but it rests on the premise that risk-reduction activities take place in the latter stages of the development process. In fact, the entire product development process needs to be managed in such a way as to reduce risk to acceptable levels by the time the launch phase is reached.

Conclusion

This chapter has analysed how each of the key product development activities is managed in high achiever and less successful product developer businesses. The overview clearly shows that high achiever businesses manage product improvements in a different way from new product developments. In the following chapters we examine these tasks separately: chapter 6 deals in detail with the management of product improvements, chapter 7 deals with the intricacies of managing new product developments.

The examples given in this chapter have shown how successful product development requires the application of teamwork throughout the whole of the development process. Such teamwork involves a critical mix of marketing and technical skills, frequently accompanied by widespread interfunctional involvement which requires effective co-ordination. The following key points summarize the findings.

A Planning product changes

- There are important differences between high and lower achiever businesses in *skill, co-ordination* and *participation* for both product improvement and new product development activities.
- Important differences were also recorded between product

improvement and new product development for the high achievers for *staff specialization, co-ordination* and *participation*. This reflects the difference in approach adopted for the two main types of product development in high achiever firms.

- The differences between high achiever and less successful businesses reflect the top-down, short-term, budget-based product planning procedures commonly found in less successful businesses.
- High achievers, as well as being strategy-led and market-led, usually have a more structured product planning framework, evidenced by regular meetings attended by top management which provide a clear message that product planning is regarded as important. In these firms new product development planning involves fewer specialists (commonly only marketing and technical), is less co-ordinated (via written procedures) and actually involves less persons (possibly due to the commercially sensitive nature of new product development) than does planning for product improvements.
- The *co-ordination* scores are significantly higher in more successful businesses, yet show an important difference between product improvement (high) and new product development (low). This provides further evidence of the 'loose-tight' methods of operation adopted in high achiever businesses. Planning market-based new product development opportunities is a 'loose' existential activity, which is nevertheless contained within 'tight' overall strategies. Planning product improvements is much less of an unknown area, and so can be more tightly co-ordinated.

B Idea exploration

- Important differences were found for *all* new product activities between high achiever and less successful businesses, but only minor differences for product improvement. Successful businesses distinguish themselves in the way they explore ideas for possible new products.
- They do so first and foremost because their new product development is market-led rather than constrained by technological or other supply-side factors. It therefore requires a relatively unconstrained ('loose') approach during the idea exploration stage. In contrast, the exploration of ideas for product improvements is

far more circumscribed in both successful and less successful businesses.

C Screening and evaluation

- There are important differences in nearly all respects between high and lower achievers.
- While co-ordination was marginally tighter for both product improvement and new product developments in less successful firms, this masks a most important difference in approach. Less successful businesses have a propensity to *co-ordinate* screening activities during an early one-off 'snapshot' decision, rather than regarding screening and evaluation as an ongoing process, as is the common practice in successful businesses.
- *Top control* is much higher in successful firms, indicating senior managers' acceptance of responsibility for the success of particular developments.
- *Skills* are scored higher for successful firms because, in them, different hurdle rates are commonly applied to developments having different risk profiles. Less successful businesses frequently apply the same evaluative criteria to projects that bear different degrees of risk. This is clearly a less realistic way of appraising the likely value of quite different projects.

D Physical development

- Important differences were recorded between high achiever businesses and lower achievers for nearly all activities for both product improvements and for new product developments.
- High achiever businesses use self-managing interfunctional development teams for new product work which registers as a higher *skills* score. The higher *participation* scores indicate a more developed team approach in these firms.
- The higher *co-ordination* scores for the high achievers reflect the more rigorous monitoring against milestones in order to move into full production as quickly as possible.
- In high achiever businesses there are some important differences between product improvement and new product development activities. *Top control* is lower for improvement work because this is commonly delegated. However, for new product developments,

top management in successful firms takes direct interest, and also provides direct support.

E Launch

- The only differences registered for this phase between high achiever and less successful businesses were in *skills* (higher in successful businesses for new product development) and *co-ordination* (higher for product improvements and new product developments). The fact that far fewer operational differences were recorded during this activity is not really surprising because all firms take product launches seriously.
- In the high achiever businesses the only important difference between product improvement and new product development was in *top control.* This can be explained by a greater propensity on the part of top management to delegate improvement tasks, as was noted under physical development.

The following two chapters build on the straight reporting of results by exploring qualitatively and prescriptively the practices which underpin (1) effective product improvement and (2) new product development.

6

Effective Product Improvement Practice

THE two previous chapters demonstrated top management's contribution to product development strategies and the role of teamwork in the successful execution of development projects. These two critical factors lie at the heart of the managerial dynamics effecting product change within an organization. The objective of this chapter and the next is to explore these issues in the context of their specific application to the work of product improvement and new product development. It has been stressed throughout that product change embraces a variety of options which have different mixes of 'newness'. We shall show that in their application to specific product development options, top management's contribution and teamwork activities need to be tailored accordingly.

This chapter explores how the 7Ss (described in chapter 3) manifest themselves in the execution of projects designed to improve current products. This is done by letting managers speak for themselves: their comments provide the most telling insight into the 'how' of product change. But first it is necessary to reiterate the importance of product improvement. As will be shown, far from being viewed as a simple 'maintenance' task, product improvement constitutes a major strategic tool in the achievement of competitive advantages.

The strategic importance of product improvement

Product improvement, the redevelopment of existing products and extensions of current product lines, is an often underrated form of product change. Companies that are proud of their technical skills will sometimes shun product improvement in favour of pursuing new product lines embracing the very latest technology. This often results in over-engineered and over-priced products which are out of tune with customer demand. Product improvement is of vital importance. It is necessary for survival in increasingly competitive market environments. It can also be instrumental in rejuvenating businesses and generating profits that can be used to fund newer and more risky developments.

In large, stable and mature markets, the traditional business approach is to cut the costs of manufacture, rejecting product change as unnecessary and ineffectual. However, under the cover of stability, so-called mature markets can often be very volatile. This phenomenon is illustrated by comments made in two very different industries:

We are dealing with a mature market where the volume has been unchanged for decades ... but nowadays a lot of switches are taking place within different sectors of the market and product development is now especially important.

Marketing Manager, UK Food Products Company

Some product groups in North America have become little more than commodity items. This is not necessary, and has generally come about through a lack of innovative, aggressive, value-added marketing.

Division Head, UK Agro-Chemicals Company

Many apparently stable markets are becoming increasingly fragmented or demassified. In such circumstances, segmenting the product offering through remodelled products and improvements, targeted at varied market needs, is necessary. Even firms in traditional commodity markets, like coffee and tea, have found that treating the core product as a cash cow can lead to market share erosion. New varieties of products – designed to capture the increasing variety demanded by consumers – have enabled companies in some market segments to step outside commodity trading conditions, with their attendant narrow margins and low profits.

It is important to see that the under-the-surface turbulent nature of some mature markets has not necessarily been the result of customers clamouring for product variants. Rather, it has resulted from a few firms having the vision to seek out subtle differences in customer needs and to design a whole array of differentiated products to meet those needs. This kind of aggressive segmentation is particularly apparent in the food industry, where some companies have pursued a high growth strategy by building up a diversified portfolio of premium quality food products to meet the lifestyle needs of consumers:

There have been even fewer new brands in the last five years. We are launching products for particular sectors of the market, picking up health or taste characteristics. There's now a whole series of products that can be launched within a brand. The effort in recent years has gone on this type of range extension, not on new brands.

Marketing Manager, UK Food Products Company

We have to spend such a high proportion of our time on product development because our markets are changing so fast and are rapidly fragmenting. We have very good competitors who are very good at reading the marketplace. So we are forced to do a lot of product development.

Marketing Manager, US Food Products Company

It is in mature and apparently stable markets that product improvement can become a critical means of gaining competitive advantage. Firms that have seized the initiative, and sought to differentiate their product offerings, have become leaders in a new competitive game. An aggressive approach to product improvement has enabled some firms to rejuvenate core businesses previously viewed as being in decline. Treated as targets for cost cutting and disinvestment, which in turn leads to a spiral of lower profits and less powerful product offerings, such businesses had become a major barrier to development and growth in the firm as a whole. In many cases, the approach resulted from a misalignment of existing products with evolving market needs. While aggregate volumes may be static, the nature of customer needs change and give rise to opportunities:

We have proved that we can increase sales through imaginative product development, even in our traditional business areas. It's been a new approach to product development which has breathed life into the traditional area. It has encouraged product development to be more venturesome, less conservative, safe and incremental.

V-P Strategy & Development, US Food Products Company

Often, rejuvenation through product improvement in core businesses is based on identifying the key attributes of current products, and testing how far these dimensions might be stretched:

Our 'X' business is thirty years old and by anyone's standard, approaching a mature position. If we hadn't done anything about it, we would have gone into the ageing process. What we've been able to do is significantly upgrade the market potential of these products through continuing research. We have been able to increase the physical performance characteristics without increasing the price. This has put us into new markets. We have bought another twenty years of healthy life for the business through continuing renewal research.

Director, Departmental Plans, US Chemical Company

The message from these insights is that businesses viewed at best as cash cows, at worst as being in decline, often have considerable mileage for growth. Such mileage can be extracted by a careful development of current products in alignment with evolving market needs. As a result, core businesses are revitalized rather than pushed into decline by unimaginative management policies.

As with markets, stability and maturity in product technology can be deceptive. In such circumstances, the opportunities for product change appear to be marginal. Technological development is therefore often confined to process improvements targeted at reducing costs. But developments in process technology can be instrumental in generating opportunities for improved products. Again it comes down to the firm's approach and ability to recognize that an imaginative use of process technology can help it produce better product offerings:

The technology changes very fast, despite the fact that the product has been around for a long time. The change is in processes: this leads to cost advantages, but can also have a significant effect on product properties.

R&D Manager, UK Chemical Company

New process technology has allowed us to offer lots of product variants now. Also, we are able to simulate traditional baking skills which had departed from the industry.

Technical Manager, UK Food Products Company

These firms are actively pursuing process developments to give them opportunities for additional new product variants, as well as cost-of-manufacture benefits. For them, process and product development are inextricably intertwined and both are used creatively.

Apart from the ability to generate competitive advantage and corporate rejuvenation, product improvement holds a trump card over other types of product change: done well, it can quickly yield profits. By its very nature, it draws on the firm's current skills, be they in technology, manufacturing or marketing. It is no surprise that leading Japanese companies concentrate most of their efforts on product improvement:

When it comes to developing products, Western companies will always say: we're the first with this product. The Japanese will always approach product innovation saying: how much money can we make out of it? Anyone can have ideas, and there's no point in pushing back technical frontiers if you can't make any money. The Japanese nearly all do product line development. They say there's a great risk in doing all this new product development.

Marketing Manager, Office Products, Japanese Electronics Company

With this approach, many Japanese companies have successfully captured major market shares in industries such as consumer durables, machine tools and motorcycles – all apparently low growth, mature industries. It is a mistake to interpret the Japanese approach to product development as being simply 'me too'. Their real strength lies in the ability to continually upgrade, improve and develop current products. Initially picking up a competitor's 'new' product concept, they will try, not only to make it more cheaply, but add new and more effective features to it. Video recorders are a good example of this, where product attributes such as freeze-frame, infrared remote control and 14-day timing have been successively added to the basic product, with improved models being launched on a very regular basis.

The car industry is another good example of the Japanese approach. After securing an initial bridgehead into this marketplace on a cost basis, leading Japanese companies quickly began to use new features and add-ons incorporated into the basic price to protect and develop their market position. British and American manufacturers were slow to adopt this approach, and have continued to pursue a policy of designing-out cost through feature reduction in bottom-of-the-range models. For the Japanese, adding value through product features has been instrumental in developing market dominance in many market segments. In short, the Japanese have captured the very essence of product improvement: done well, it can continually bolster and extend market share whilst being essentially low risk and often, low cost.

While, as has been demonstrated, product improvement is vital to sustain competitive advantage, even in mature industries, companies which only pursue this type of development invariably find themselves in trouble. In the long run, simply improving or extending existing product lines is unlikely to secure survival. Industries and markets can quite rapidly disappear through radical advances in technology, often originating outside the traditional industry. To have a strategy for product change that is over-focused on current customers and markets is dangerous. Product improvement needs to be balanced by efforts to develop new products.

Managing product improvements using the 7Ss

Having argued the importance of product improvement, how can it be managed effectively and successfully? Returning to our central schema of analysis, box 6.1 summarizes, under each of the 7S headings, the key managerial factors which are instrumental in successful product improvement. It will be noted that management style and shared values appear under the remit of top management.

Box 6.1   Key factors in managing product improvements successfully

---

Top management's direct responsibilities
- **Strategy:** Strategies for product improvement should be explicit and proactive.
- **Style:*** Top management needs to adopt a supportive, sponsoring role.
- **Shared values:*** For swift and efficient progress, everyone involved should feel 'ownership' of the project.
- **Structure of task group:** A multi-functional team of line managers is needed to manage and progress product improvement projects.

Teamwork aspects
- **Staff:** Staff with good basic administrative and organizing capabilities are highly valued.
- **Skills:** Marketing skills of product management, market niching and segmentation are of great importance.
- **Systems:** The product improvement process needs thorough but not over-rigid procedures to guide it.

---

* Shared values and management style appear under the remit of top management. While the effects of these two factors manifest themselves in teamworking, they result from top management's actions.

As chapters 3 and 5 show, while the effects of style and shared values manifest themselves in teamworking, their causes lie in top management action. For the purposes of understanding the 7Ss of product change in an applied sense, it is therefore necessary to examine what top management does (style) to ensure widespread acceptance of the importance of product improvement efforts within the organization as a whole (shared values).

The rest of this chapter examines and explores each of the factors in turn. As the analysis unfolds, it will be seen that each of the 7Ss interrelates with the others. For instance, an appropriate team may be set up for carrying out product improvement projects but, without the right kind of top management support, it is unlikely that it will ever be able to operate effectively. Our examination of how to manage product improvement successfully draws on examples from firms that are accomplished product developers, as well as from those that are struggling to master this task. The analysis builds on the straight reporting of our research results by focusing on prescription: how to carry out product improvement. Wherever possible, we have let managers speak for themselves.

Top management's role

We deal first with strategy, style, shared values and the structure of the task group used to pursue product improvements. In all of this, top management has a key role to play. It is top management who should take the lead in framing the firm's product improvement strategy. It needs to provide the right kind of support. Top management also has a key role to play in inculcating an acceptance at all levels of the organization of the need for product change. Finally, it must commission the right kind of task group to execute improvements.

An explicit product development strategy

A frequent mistake made by companies that are less successful at pursuing product improvement is to let development work trundle on without any strategic impetus or direction. In short, product improvement efforts are carried out in a strategic vacuum. The necessity for having a clear strategy is no less important for updating current products than with any other type of product change. There are several reasons for this. Product improvement work is more often than not disruptive of current activities and can be costly. These problems manifest themselves particularly in the tension between production efficiency and production flexibility.

Ensuring that the manufacturing capacity of the company has the ability to produce new product variants and also the ability to respond to change without incurring severe added costs requires skilful management of the relationship between existing and updated products. Clear objectives and targets are required to allow managers to weigh the importance of efficiency in current business operations against the need for modified products. Lack of enthusiasm from the manufacturing function to take on product improvements was frequently cited by managers as a key inhibitor of product change. Given a lack of strategic direction, it is hardly surprising that the manufacturing arm of a firm is reluctant to take on work that is in direct conflict with its own efficiency goals.

The dangers of letting customers dictate

As well as the costs and disruption involved, other factors combine to make an explicit strategy for product improvement a necessity. Where a firm is engaging in product improvement without clear aims and objectives, it frequently allows customers to dictate the development program. At first sight this seems eminently sensible; after all, almost every study into product development demonstrates that meeting customer needs is the key requisite of success.

There is, however, a subtle and telling difference between developing profitable products that meet marketplace needs and developing products that simply please individual customers. Without a clear strategy for product improvement, a firm can easily fall into the trap of producing a new product variant each time a customer suggests one. What often results is an over-blown product range which is expensive to manage and incorporates many unprofitable or low volume products. We spoke to an R & D manager in a UK chemical company who berated his firm's lack of strategy for product improvement:

It's the manager serving a customer who makes the most noise that gets his product on the range.

Firms which allow customers to suggest product developments for them have the delusion that, by doing so, they are market led. In fact they are sales-led. Only information on current products from current customers is collected (usually on an *ad hoc* basis) via the sales force and no overall assessment is made in respect to aggregate market needs. This in turn leads the firm to be product-led in its approach to product change:

The push behind changes will come from the Marketing Department which will be monitoring sales performance. When that starts to dip we will then check how the product compares with our competitors, and if it's appearance that seems to be wrong, we will look at that. Then, if the product is fairly old in its life and it is beginning to stutter, we will look for a replacement.

Marketing Manager, U K White Goods Company

In my opinion, we do not have a sufficiently structured approach to identifying new product modifications. I have made myself unpopular from time to time for suggesting that we do not redesign as much as refine our products in reaction to external demands like lower noise levels, higher speed, etc. This has led to a procession of rather safe product modifications of a minor nature.

Technical Director, U S Mechanical Engineering Company

One American firm we visited recalled how this product-led approach to product improvement had actively pushed one of its businesses into decline:

It took us a year and a fresh perspective to see that this business was not maturing; yet we had performance results that said it was. This was a revelation to us: we had thought that the world of engineering polymers revolved only around the sorts of products we produced. But what had happened was that most of our competitors had conceded these markets to us and there were other markets that we had completely missed. Our competitors had moved on to another performance curve. We had not perceived that these guys were competing with us because they were not producing products like ours.

Director, Departmental Plans, U S Chemical Company

This firm realized that rather than being customer-led or product-led, it had to be market-led in its approach to product improvement. In doing so it changed the whole strategic perspective of the business in question from an ageing one into a growth one. In this, it is often the customers who do not currently purchase a firm's products that can give the greatest insight into the kind of product improvement which is needed to secure continuing growth.

Sitting back and waiting for customers to suggest ideas for product improvements can also often mean that a firm is not the most 'innovative' in its market. In this, it is important to understand two things about customers. First, that the majority of customers, industrial and consumer, are likely to be conservative. They will dislike changing from tried and trusted products – in the same way that many manufacturers find product change uncomfortable. Secondly, customers very often do not have the technical information or general vision to articulate precisely the product changes that they would find most useful.

Given these considerations, a firm which solely follows customer initiatives is only likely to become as good as the customer is at responding to change, which, in some instances, is not very good at all:

Our customers give us a performance envelope and we then try and match it. ... Having said that, our biggest growth area was when we made a breakthrough which we invented and patented.

Technical Director, U K Rubber Components Company

It is most important for a firm to understand that its own innovative vision directly influences its achievement in product change. In many industrial markets, where it is certainly necessary to work closely with customers, it becomes critically important to identify leading edge customers if a firm wants to pursue a vigorous program of product change:

We are very much the servant of other people's marketing programs. So the trick is to pick the right customers to do business with. Once we are hitched to them, we are entirely dependent on them for our business.

General Manager, UK Paint Company

I will be putting more and more of my people at the customer interface. I shall be asking them to go to our stronger lead customers. These lead customers can provide us with the insights we need.

R&D Vice-President, U S Rubber Components Company

Of course we are not advocating that ideas from customers are ignored – far from it. Current customers are, however, only able to provide limited insights into the overall need for product improvement. A firm needs to make a proper assessment of the market, incorporating an understanding of both current and potential customers, from which a clear strategy for product improvement can be derived. It needs to identify leading-edge customers and work closely with them. It cannot and should not allow its current customers to have the first and last word about what products are to be developed.

Allowing competitors to seize the initiative

The other community, to which the strategic initiative for product improvement naturally gravitates in the absence of an explicit strategy, is competitors. Many companies simply wait to see what competitors bring out, or are forced into responding because of an erosion of market share:

A customer comes along and says our material is uncompetitive among other suppliers or even a replacement material. We are then obliged to find a new formulation or a way for modifying the product. There is therefore a degree of product innovation in terms of new formulations to overcome the drawbacks of our products compared with those of competitors.

Technical Manager, UK Chemicals Company

When I go down to the research department I always come back dissatisfied, in particular because the objectives the technical people have agreed with marketing are so woolly. Also, that the objectives are not stretching enough ... they are aiming solely for parity with the competition.

Division Head, UK Agro-Chemicals Company

It is important not to confuse these examples with a proactive strategy of 'fast-followership'. These companies have an *ad hoc* approach to product improvement, engaging in developments when, by chance, they become aware of competitors' offerings. In such circumstances, a firm is always going to be behind its major competitors in product development. As the Japanese have demonstrated, fast followership – quickly copying, launching and improving upon competitors' products – can be highly successful in some marketplaces. But to be successful, such an approach needs to be underpinned by an explicit strategy, formulated on the basis of a structured monitoring of competitive moves and countermoves.

In other words, the company still controls the initiative for its product improvement efforts, despite the fact that it launches second or third into a market.

Managing the development program

Apart from the activities of customers and competitors, there are managerial reasons why an explicit strategy for product improvement is necessary. Invariably a firm has more ideas for product improvement than it can logistically handle. Without a clear strategy, a firm has no means of telling which projects make the most business sense to pursue:

There is a tendency to put out a grade very quickly. There is little control over the number of grades on the range, so we grow exponentially. What we have is 'grade range inflation'.

Technical Manager, U K Chemicals Company

In this example, the company has ended up with an over-blown product range which is expensive and difficult to manage. It is a trap that firms whose products (in this case, chemical compounds) are easy to manipulate, add to and modify are likely to fall into. By the same token, following up ideas without any strategic direction can lead to developing product modifications which are incompatible with the current product range or which cannibalize the sales of current products.

These issues demonstrate that even proposals for minor product improvements need to be related to an overall product development plan. The plan should recognize the strengths and nature of current product lines in relation to market opportunities. Without a strategy, whether the firm likes it or not, the activities of customers and competitors will combine to shape its product improvement program by default.

Formulating a strategy for product improvement

Having argued for the importance of a clear strategy for product improvement, how should it be formulated? All strategies for product change need to be firmly embedded in corporate strategy. It is the latter which determines the strategic arenas the firm wants and needs to be in, and the contribution that is looked for from the firm's product development program. It is not surprising that many of the firms we visited that did not have a clear product development strategy also lack the most cursory of corporate strategies. Not only is it vital to have the product development strategy incorporated into, and flowing out from, the corporate strategy for proper resource allocation, but this is also important for 'psychological' reasons. Elevating product development as a central element of corporate strategy gives the task mainstream credibility.

The second ground rule for product development strategy is that it should, whenever possible, aim for broadly defined markets. Markets need to be conceptualized in many different ways, of which geography is only one. With regard to geography, some of our sample firms had a pronounced 'home-county' approach to business in general, and their marketing and product improvement strategies in particular. Several factors may make it necessary to pursue a wider global approach to product development, even in the case of developments to the current product line. The high costs of development may mean that domestic markets are not big enough to generate sufficient return. These problems appear to be particularly acute in Britain. It was noticeable that firms that complain that their troubles are rooted in the contraction of the British manufacturing base often persist in only developing products geared for the domestic market. Unfortunately, even though some of these firms have now begun to realize that they must somehow compete in the broader global market, they no longer have the skills, infrastructure or resources to do so effectively.

The comments of a manager in a British subsidiary of a Japanese company shed light on the problems of restricting product development horizons to limited marketplaces:

Almost all of our new products are geared to making it in the Japanese market. Bear in mind, the scale of that market is incredible. We know that if it can't survive there, it will die anyway. In Britain, in a booming market, we might be selling 50,000 fax machines a year – in Japan, we would sell 1 million. It's a market of 110 million people – half the size of the US in a much smaller area – and it's more competitive than any other market.

Marketing Manager, Office Products, Japanese Electronics Company

This manager described the European and North American markets as 'tame' by comparison and this partly explains why the Japanese have had such success in these markets. If a product holds up in the vibrant and highly competitive Japanese market, then the rest of the world often provides easy pickings.

It is important to see that the need to globalize the approach to product development is not simply applicable to industrial markets. Food manufacturers will regularly cite short shelf lives and the complexities of distribution as reasons for not going global. Yet foreign, particularly European, competitors have made considerable inroads into, for instance, the British market for dairy products. In the face of such threats, a typical reaction from many British companies is to offer to factor competitors' goods in the home market.

There is evidence, however, that some British companies are beginning to reorientate their business towards a more global stance:

We want to go more international: only part of our business is international. The major groups in the world are massing in this way, but we are still only a niche player.

Marketing Manager, U K Paint Company

What we are up against is increasing development spend in high technology. ... With the centre of the company always wanting a contribution, we must link up international markets.

Technical Director, U K Electronic Engineering Company

Another central tenet of product improvement strategy is that it looks further ahead than a year. This long-term view is an obvious necessity for new product development, but is also applicable for product improvement. This is because improving products can be a long and involved process, and also because, in many marketplaces, a longer-term horizon for product improvement can itself trigger the identification of opportunities for more radical developments. Firms that only look as far as their next development allow their product improvement programs to become project orientated rather than geared to the evolving demands of selected markets.

A key input into product development strategy is marketing information. High achieving firms spend a lot of time and money on assessing marketplaces. They keep in close and constant touch with current leading-edge customers and carry out research into customer groupings which they do not currently serve. Monitoring competitors is likewise intensive. There is no secret formula for success: high achievers simply apply themselves to developing a thorough and ongoing understanding of their marketplaces. Such an understanding yields product and market opportunities and provides early warning signals that current product ranges are becoming out of tune with customer demands and competitive conditions. For less successful product developers, the cost of such wide-ranging market research appears to be an anathema. Yet they will quite happily pursue product improvements which absorb substantial development funds on the basis of the most cursory and incomplete market information. Clearly, marketing expenditure, as with technical resources, is an investment – not a cost – when it comes to successful product development:

It is clear to me, but I have not been able to convince people here, that in mature products we might innovate in the channels of distribution. But we lack a marketing director to point out the potential benefits. In my opinion, the lack of a strategic market analysis is costing us money – it's an opportunity cost. In my opinion, we could make more money than we do at present.

R&D Director, US Electronic Engineering Company

Companies that we found to be adept at product improvement aim to renew a certain percentage of their current products regularly. In successful companies, this kind of aggressive product improvement stems from a complex strategy setting process. In Hewlett-Packard we found that senior managers spend upwards of a third of their time in strategy formulation. For this purpose, inputs are sought from technical and marketing specialists and also from managers of business units operating in related areas. The information is in turn reconciled with the strategic mission of the company as a whole. The complex process generates:

- the specific aims and objectives for the product improvement program,
- criteria by which top management checks product improvement progress

Hence, in Hewlett-Packard, strategy formulation is a cyclical process in which development plans are continually evolved, assessed and renewed in the light of updated information.

Another American company, this time in the chemical industry, pursued a less centralized approach to product improvement strategy. Business units are encouraged to formulate their own plans for product improvement based on their assessment of the markets they operate in. Each business unit has a specialist planner who also reports to the central planning function. Each month the businesses have formal strategic reassessment reviews with the central planners in which the business unit's interpretation of its own competitive position is discussed along with the strategies needed to improve that position.

From these discussions, development programs are devised and resources released. This process runs alongside the more traditional profit and loss performance monitoring, so the business unit manager is measured on his short-term activity as well as his longer-term improvement plans. The central planning function in this company does not perceive its role as a dictator of plans. Rather, it acts as catalyst and coach, allowing each business unit to use its intimate knowledge of the marketplace to formulate effective plans for product improvement.

We found the same kind of strategic process going on in some British companies:

The system we have now lays down two years ahead what products are to be developed. Major enhancements are foreseen three years ahead of launch. It's the market opportunities that are planned for. How we meet that opportunity technically is another matter

Technical Director, UK Electronic Engineering Company

Companies such as these believe that strategies for product improvement need to be explicit; thought through by all participants, and rooted in a sound analysis of the marketplace. Accordingly, they have detailed plans, identify projects, development resources and market objectives for specific product markets. The strategy provides the focus for idea generation, so that ideas are suggested that capitalize on specific market opportunities identified by the strategy formulation process. The strategic objectives also provide the key criteria on which a project is screened when the development process unwinds. The strategy helps the firm prioritize projects, making sure that limited resources are applied in the right areas. In this way strategy becomes the driving force behind the product improvement process.

Effective managerial styles for product improvement

An explicit strategy for product improvement provides the framework within which all participants can develop an understanding of their contribution to the firm's development efforts. It is then incumbent upon senior management to adopt a managerial style which facilitates and supports the effective implementation of strategy. When talking about top management in this context, we mean those senior managers involved in making the key strategic decisions for specific businesses. Depending on the organization and policies of the company, this may mean the CEO and his board team, or the head of a business unit.

The actions of top management have a vital bearing on the outcomes of all kinds of product change activity. This is no less so for product improvement; particularly, as will be seen later, it is best carried out by managers who are at a fairly low level in the organization. Product change is, by its very nature, a multi-functional activity requiring the interplay of the firm's many skill bases. Top level support is required to facilitate and promote projects, sometimes arbitrating between varied inputs. Throughout the study, it was found that a lack of top management support was frequently singled out by managers as a key reason for a poor development record. Several times project managers mentioned that the way to speed up development – a crucial issue – is to have explicit top management support.

But simply to say that product development needs top management support is insufficient. It is the nature of that support that is all important. It will be shown that the kind of support necessary for product improvement is subtly different from that required for new product development. For product improvement, top management must seek to create the right kind of managerial environment which allows middle and lower management to get on with the nuts and bolts of the task in hand, while providing the necessary support at critical stages in the process. We have found that the type of management style that best facilitates product improvement is best summed up as 'supportive sponsorship'.

Laissez-faire or authoritarian management

As with most of the issues involved in the management of product improvement, as much can be learnt from examples of how top management should not approach the task, as from examples of how they should. In the companies where we found product improvement being haphazardly and ineffectively carried out, two types of top management style were apparent. The top managers of these companies either adopt a *laissez-faire* approach to product improvement activities, or an authoritarian one.

The *laissez-faire* style of top manager will simple delegate all responsibility for product development to lower management where it typically gets lost in the plethora of other work:

On the assumption that this will not find its way upstairs, the amount of direct involvement by a CEO in product development depends on the man. The last CEO we had was a marketing man and he had a dominating influence. The man we have now has come out of the financial area and is not so active in steering the product development program. And for better or for worse, the level of administrative attention given to product development has diminished.

Technical Manager, U S Mechanical Engineering Firm

In this particular company, top managers did not assist in unplugging the bottlenecks or resource conflicts that invariably occur between the different functions and business units involved in development work. It is in just such an environment that the firm has to rely on self-styled product champions. Without their strong personal commitment to and enthusiastic and sometimes bloody-minded support for a project, many product developments would simply not have materialized:

I believe we lack a marketing thrust and I am going to designate individuals as New Opportunity Technologists or something like that and get them out into the market. I may be totally wrong in this, but I believe I am taking the responsibility of the General Manager of the Division. If he abdicates that responsibility, someone else has to take it on. ... If the President really wanted all the businesses to concentrate more on product development, he could lay down a target saying we want *x* per cent of sales revenue from new products developed in the next *y* years. That is one way of focusing on what's important. It's a way of saying: 'I am expecting you to grow your business.' I personally would rather have the interest and the pressure from the top rather than trying to drum up the pressure all the time.

R&D Vice President, US Rubber Components Company

As far as motivating people to be more innovative is concerned, I think people at the top of the company have to take more of an interest. If I were running the company, I would bring in product managers and I would make it clear that I want the company to grow. At present, we don't have regular briefings with top managers.

R&D Manager, US Mechanical Engineering Company

For a business to rely on a few exceptional individuals to force change through the inertia created by an uninterested top management is a high-risk approach, where much is left to chance and to the personalities involved. From our investigations, we became convinced that undiluted product championing is a symptom of a failed management, rather than, as is commonly believed, evidence of a healthy climate for development activities.

A no more effective, though quite different style of top management for product improvement can be described as authoritarian. The authoritarian style top manager will likewise delegate all responsibility for development work, but will crucially retain the power to veto a project at any stage of its development, almost on a whim. Support does not seem to be forthcoming from this manager, only demands for evidence of progress. In several of the less successful firms we came across this style of top management. The result was that product improvement was reluctantly or haphazardly carried out. It is difficult to overstate the frustration of managers in these firms:

I was put in as a product champion, whatever that means. There was a big fanfare about it. But I was not manager status and I was having to ask managers of other departments to co-operate. But no one was backing me ... I had a mandate from the directors ... but the directors didn't want to get into the mud and sort it out. It was always 'I told you to do it, now ... where are we?'

Engineer, UK Mechanical Engineering Company

We had a brand which, to all intents and purposes, was not successful. It was launched as a result of over-commitment and then there's someone at my level having to go to the Chairman and say it won't work and he says 'what have you got wrong?' ... You need to choose your words very carefully when presenting projects to top management and stress that things are only at a very early stage, and not allow the baby to be thrown out with the bath water.

New Product Development Manager, UK Food Company

Both of these severely inhibiting top management styles can be traced to one source: risk averseness. Product development of any kind is risky and, in many instances, no one person feels more personal risk than the top manager:

I have worked in other parts of this company where there was a lack of enthusiasm for change from the top. There was more concern about the problems change would bring rather than the opportunities it would present.

Division Head, UK Packaging Company

In both managerial cases, the risk involved in product improvement is off-loaded on to lower functional managers. The whimsical veto of authoritarian style managers exercised at any point in the development process is a classic symptom of insecurity. These top managers appear to suddenly become aware of the development resources absorbed by projects. They then seek to exert *ad hoc* control over outcomes, without having ensured that the necessary inputs (resources, skills and staff) are in place.

Both types of manager are actually compounding development risks, especially in cases where an explicit strategy for product improvement has not been formulated. In such circumstances, the initiative for product improvement is left to managers lower in the organization who have little or no understanding of where the business as a whole needs to go. In exceptional cases, product champions may emerge who push particular developments according to their own idiosyncratic or functional perspectives. However, the first rule of risk reduction should, in our opinion, be to identify the variables that are controllable, and the starting point of such control is the framing of an explicit product development strategy.

Sponsoring by top management

In stark contrast, top management in firms that are high achievers in product improvement adopt a managerial style which allows them to be supportive of development efforts while letting the managers closest to the work get on with it:

The MD gets involved in product development in a whole series of formal and informal meetings. But he is not a peerless leader in the old mill-owner syndrome mould. He never takes control of my job, but he does take a very close interest.

Marketing Manager, UK Mechanical Engineering Company

It is important to note that an explicit strategy for product improvement allows top management to adopt this kind of facilitating role. It allows it to relinquish day-to-day control over particular projects. Excessive control would invariably hinder the speed with which product improvement is undertaken, with much energy being absorbed by staff in briefing senior managers on progress and problems. Instead, in these firms, senior managers exert control via the clear strategic objectives against which progress is checked:

Bob keeps in touch almost weekly and has a good feel for where we are – much more than top managers in other companies I've worked for. Once top management is committed by signing off the first checkpoint we know we've all got the support we need.

R&D Project Manager, US Electronic Engineering Company

The CEO spends 5 per cent of his time checking product development. He has delegated product development activities, but has control procedures in place to ensure that the work is being done efficiently.

Project Manager, US Food Products Company

Operating within a clear strategic frame of reference, top management can and does delegate both the right level of responsibility and the right level of authority to those involved in managing and progressing individual projects. Top management in these companies perceives its role as one of sponsoring the firm's product improvement program. It will check progress against strategic objectives and will act as troubleshooter, unknotting resource conflicts and identifying skill shortages or manpower difficulties. It acts as a powerful back-up to those considered most capable of dealing with the nuts and bolts of product improvement: the managers closest to individual marketplaces. As such, top management can be viewed as the champion of product improvement activity, rather than simply another player which development staff have to satisfy in the pursuit of particular projects. In summary, top managers in high achiever firms confine their direct involvement in product improvement to three areas:

- Responsibility in setting the strategic direction of the product improvement program.
- Endowing the task group with the right level of authority within the organization.
- At crucial points, ensuring that the work being carried out is meeting strategic objectives.

Shared ownership

One of the prerequisites for successful product change is an acceptance within all levels of the organization of the need for such change. Product development of any kind invariably requires inputs from many parts of the organization and from many skill bases. If any one of these elements does not share the belief in the project's necessity, progress will be inhibited. In the case of product improvement, which directly implicates current operations, everyone in the company will be involved in, or affected by the project. It is of vital importance that, even when not directly involved in shaping a project, each group within the firm feels some kind of shared commitment to, or ownership of it:

The reason you get high performance from people is because they feel that their personal aims are linked with the aims of the business. The role of upper management is twofold: first, to support and endorse the vision so that its organizational importance is clear; second, to support it with resources. ... In this way, individuals have a high sense of identity of purpose. They feel free to contribute the full range of their abilities. So, values, beliefs, worth and purpose are far more important initially for development than specialist skills. You can take low levels of skills and still have success, but you can't have success with low levels of motiviation.

Director, Business Development, US Food Products Company

In this company, top management explicitly recognized that product improvement requires a cross-functional commitment which cannot be generated by the design of the organization itself, but by management actions and approach. In companies that were less successful at product improvement we invariably found the 'not invented here' syndrome rearing its head. The comments of a technical manager of a British mechanical engineering firm are typical and demonstrate just how harmful this attitude can be:

People in the Design & Development Department used to say: 'Let's look at what this looks like ... '. We kicked it around for a while and quite often we'd go 60 per cent down the road before we could get other departments interested in it. The manufacturing people had a quiet life, making things they knew all about. They didn't want to hear about alterations: change was not a thing they welcomed.

This manager felt that one of the first things needed to improve his firm's performance was to address the issue of shared commitment to product improvement.

Instilling shared values or, in the case of product improvement, shared ownership of development projects in a company is not easy. It is this element of our schema which really demonstrates how interrelated the 7Ss are. Shared ownership is generated by several factors working together. An explicit strategy for product improvement communicates formally to managers the importance of product change activities. As we have seen, top management needs to underpin this with the correct type of supportive management style which both lends credence to the strategy and actively demonstrates ongoing support for it. Correct strategy and an appropriate management style are, therefore, prerequisites for the inculcation of shared ownership at all levels of the firm.

In some high achieving firms we found management had introduced various staff development policies specifically designed to encourage the right level of cross-functional commitment to project work. Sometimes these involved temporary job swapping between functions as part of general staff training, it being felt that this produces a cross-fertilization of functional perspectives. In a general sense, such training does help to develop an appreciation of corporate purpose and business mission. In a narrower sense, it helps functions co-operate effectively when they have to work together on specific product improvement projects. In some of the most experienced product developer businesses, career progress is dependent on development record:

In a company such as ours, what generally happens is the people who are successful at innovation get a chance to do it again. That's the reward. Every senior manager has a good product innovation record.

R&D Project Manager, US Electronic Engineering Company

Identifying the correct means for generating shared ownership of development projects is highly specific to the firm itself, its history and culture. Moreover, once begun, shared ownership needs to be continually nurtured in the face of changing circumstances and turnover of personnel. However, from our investigation, it is clear that one of the most effective ways for addressing the problem of shared commitment in product improvement is to ensure that as many functions as possible are formally involved in development work.

Structuring task groups

Firms that carry out large and important product improvements successfully invariably set up task groups or teams to manage individual projects or groups of related projects. We found this happening in all four sectors of the manufacturing industries researched. Despite these different industrial settings, the composition of the teams used and the way they are set up display the following common characteristics:

- Team composition is established as early as possible in the product development process.
- The team consists of a broad range of functional specialists, and always includes marketing, technical and manufacturing personnel.
- Most of the staff making up the team have worked closely with existing customers.
- Staff involved in task groups are at a relatively low managerial level within the organization.

Juggling with the issues

The reason why these firms consider teamworking so vital for efficient product improvement, and why it has proved to be so effective in many of the cases we came across, is not hard to discover. Product improvement is, by its very nature, an iterative and problem-solving process. An initial suggestion for a product update or improvement needs to be moulded and shaped into a viable product concept. This involves juggling with technical, marketing and manufacturing issues, which are invariably in conflict. A change in product attributes (a marketing input) has implications for the technical development of the product and for its manufacture. Likewise, insoluble technical problems are likely to prompt a reassessment of the market attractiveness of the product concept.

It is only by setting up a team of different functional specialists, who can sit round a table and address the many issues involved, that progress can be made with anything like the speed necessary for successful product improvement. A team provides a forum for dialogue between functional inputs in which a whole series of options and solutions can be discussed quickly.

The value of teamworking is well illustrated by the slower progress made by firms that do not set up teams to carry out product improvements. In many instances, a firm will create a separate managerial post for 'product development'. Typically, the manager involved will be located either in the technical or marketing function. The common trap that these firms fall into is the belief that, by creating a 'specialist', all the inputs required for successful product improvement will be made:

Our business, like most others, is complex. There is no way in which we could create a new product manager whose job it would be to identify all product development opportunities. Ideas for product developments come out of many diverse inputs and from many different sources. It is important to capture these inputs from production, engineering, sales and service.

Technical Manager, U K Mechanical Engineering Company

No single individual or specialist product development manager can hope to be adequately skilled in the marketing, technical, design, engineering and manufacturing issues which need to be addressed. Indeed, where a 'new' product manager is located in a particular function, he/she will inevitably adopt the predominant perspectives of that function, thereby applying an unhealthy bias to the development. We found instances where such specialist development managers decide the strategic arena for new product development, what projects pass the screening process, and also make the decision on whether a project has been properly and successfully investigated.

The complexities of product improvement mean that rarely can one designated 'new' product manager act independently. Sooner or later he/she will need to call on other functional resources. Rarely is the manager appointed at a senior management level. Usually the status of the manager is equivalent to a brand manager in the marketing function, or a project engineer in the technical function.

From this kind of level, it becomes an almost impossible task to lead the work that has to be done in different functions, over which the manager has no line authority.

In these circumstances, the fate of product improvements is left to the personalities of the people involved and 'goodwill'. Moreover, at this kind of level, a product development manager is likely to feel very vulnerable. All the responsibility for product improvement is focused on him/her. Not surprisingly, what commonly results is a stream of minor low-risk product adjustments which only have an incremental effect on the organization's operation and performance.

'Over-the-Wall'

Even in firms where the need to involve many functions in product development is accepted, what often happens is that each stage in the process is assigned to an individual function to try and push the work through existing line management systems. Typically, in technically-led firms, the technical function is given the overall responsibility for product improvement. Prompted by a technical development, a proposal for a product update or modification emerges. A lot of development work then ensues, sometimes extending over many months and the product concept is worked up to the point that it is technically feasible:

What has happened in the past was that the technical people would say: 'Well, it looks sort of good – let's pursue it a bit further.' Then they would put it into their regular organization. That is time consuming, often costly, and we sometimes have a tendency to want to perfect things before we let it move ahead. There are times when you need to bring a prototype up to a certain point so that you can really tell whether there is a market rather than getting the ultimate design. ... Our technical people do not like to put out anything unless it's 'the best!'.

R&D Manager, US Mechanical Engineering Company

The development may then get passed over to the commercial functions to find an appropriate marketplace. In this way, a lot of time and money has been spent before any effort has been made to address marketing issues:

The real snags tend to come from marketing. When they see the developed product it's often not what they expected or wanted. That's why I believe more of the initiative for developments should come from marketing. ...

It would be helpful if marketing told us what they wanted earlier ... not after we've done the work.

Chief Development Engineer, U S Mechanical Engineering Company

If 'selling' problems are encountered, the whole project, typically, gets passed back to the technical function to 'rework'. By the time it reaches the marketing arm of the company for a second or third time, developments in both the market and technology may mean that the product improvement is no longer viable.

In marketing-led firms, almost the opposite pattern may occur. An idea for an improved product gets suggested within the marketing function. A lot of work is carried out on its market potential and the precise product attributes demanded by the market are refined. Only after all the marketing issues are resolved are technical and manfacturing concerns addressed. Problems in either or both of these areas may prove insoluble, or at least require the redesign of the product offering, which in turn affects market acceptance. Again, much time and resources will have been wasted while the market may well have moved on.

These two scenarios demonstrate that there is no way of getting round the fact that product improvement is a process which requires updated marketing and technical information to be constantly fed into the process. A successful product improvement is the result of integrating all relevant factors contributing to the product, which have to be considered in parallel right from the beginning of the development process. It is simply not possible to divide the process into exclusive boxes, allowing each individual function to complete its work before the next function takes over. It is interesting that on both sides of the Atlantic, the more successful companies have a derisory term for this kind of approach to product improvement, in Britain, it is called 'pass the parcel'; in America, 'over the wall'.

Many of the firms that have persisted with this approach to product improvement have tried to solve the problems it generates by setting up a product development committee. Far from making the process more efficient, such committees often create a whole new set of problems. Usually made up of senior functional managers, the committee's role in the product development process is rarely clarified. Often committees will vary their approach, sometimes being a proactive policymaker, at other times simply acting as a co-ordinating device. In many instances, the committee itself becomes yet another bureaucratic barrier to the progress of the project, and, for those doing the work, satisfying the committee may become an end in itself. The comments of one marketing manager in a British food products company illustrate the problems:

The committee became a progress committee ... it was never very innovatory. It always took the compromise view. It was inward-looking and incestuous. It rarely addressed the market needs of the future. In the end I organized task groups for particular activities in the product development process and picked people with appropriate skills and motivation.

Marketing Manager, UK Food Products Company

Teamworking as a means for generating commitment

The 'over the wall' or 'pass the parcel' approach to product improvement is not only ineffectual because of its incompatibility with the problem-solving and iterative nature of the development process. Passing the project over the wall from function to function is counter-productive in developing the kind of commitment necessary for speedy progress through development hurdles. In firms where there is traditionally a dominant function, be it technical or marketing, other functions inevitably become reluctant service arms to that function:

Marketing are not involving us. We are not getting the feedback to tell us 'this is what we're doing and this is why we want it'. This is, however, necessary background information so that you can understand and appreciate why you're being asked to do something. The issue affects the running and motivation of the whole department. We should also move towards involving engineering and production so that we can take into account all relevant factors.

Technical Director, UK Food Products Company

'Over the wall' by its very nature produces a situation where the various functions have only a passing interest in a project's progress and success. Even where a function gets involved again further down the line, different units of that function may be drawn in. Thus, there is usually little chance for the project to generate its own status and credibility within the function's overall work. Typically there is confusion both within and between functions regarding the importance of the project:

I am very confused about whether a project has been properly looked at as to whether it's worthwhile to develop. By the time we have it we are about the third group of people to see it, and it assumes a momentum which is not necessarily a healthy one.

Technical Manager, UK Chemicals Company

It is precisely because it has the potential to generate commitment that a team approach is so effective for product improvement. It is well known that group working generates group identity, loyalty and commitment. There is a concerted interest in the success of the project and a momentum is generated that is vital to push through the problems that will occur:

Our developments come under the concept of integrated innovation – we go forward with everyone co-operating in parallel rather than a parcel being passed in series, as it were, from function to function. We used to be different.... In the past, new products were rarely shown to the manufacturing people in case the idea of disruption upset them. Now we all work together – the engineering people, the purchasing people – are all given product development responsibility.

Market Manager, UK Mechanical Engineering Company

Firms that do not use teams cited costs as one reason for not doing so. However, teamworking is not only capable of speeding up the development process but, in most cases, has the potential to reduce the costs of development. The cost of solving a manufacturing problem in the project's early stages is dramatically lower than having to solve it later on. Often, the earlier a problem is addressed, the more cheaply it can be resolved.

Teamworking in action

The full value of the team concept can best be brought out by examining some of the examples we came across. In a division of a major American electronics firm, we found that very soon after an idea was suggested a team began to form. The company allowed a team leader to emerge, usually from within the technical function. The team leader would then begin recruiting staff from different functional areas to build up the team necessary for carrying out the project:

In other companies I've worked in, there's a separate team handling the investigation and they hand the product definition to another team within the company. But here we try and have the same team of guys who have worked on the definition, working on the implementation. So we tend to form teams where the skills of the people are fairly broad. We look for people on these teams who can take an idea all the way through ... and that has advantages. You get ownership going. Ownership is very important, because as the project develops it always changes and it's best to have that team of people who were in at the start. People who really understand why we're doing this in the first place, and what the alternatives were. Because, as changes come up in the middle of the project, they have the knowledge to make appropriate decisions.

R&D Project Manager, US Electronics Company

In this firm, the 'core team' consists of a specialist from each of the key functions: marketing, technical and manufacturing. At key points in the development process, other functional specialists will be brought in to supplement the skills of those on the main team. For instance, finance specialists will be brought in at specific stages to make detailed assessments of the project's investment implications.

It is important to note that staff manning teams in this firm are at a fairly low level in the organization – lower to middle management. They have the time to address the issues involved in depth. Their apparent lack of managerial clout is offset by the fact that they have direct access to top management. At key review points the team reports directly to top management. It is then that top management can make sure that the project is proceeding well and requests for help to solve particular resource problems or conflicts can be made. Use is made of a 'program manager' post – a senior manager is appointed as a kind of sponsor of the product improvement team's work – and he helps to facilitate progress in between regular checks by top management. We found that a program manager is common where there are many product improvement teams.

In many companies we found that the person who was the prime mover behind a viable product development suggestion becomes its team leader, be they a marketing, manufacturing or technical specialist. That person is then required to build his/her own team. This ensures that the person heading the initiative is fully committed to it, and also to the team:

Someone who feels strongly about the idea who's willing to take ownership and who feels strongly enough to push it forward. They will write a document which lays the groundwork. It will say: 'this is the amount of money and time we need, and these are the type of people I need to get together to form a team.'

R&D Project Manager, U S Electronics Company

We found that teams set up to manage product improvements rarely consist of more than six people, but that staffing may be ramped-up at particular stages:

Composition of the team depends on the particular project. All projects start with a representative from marketing and engineering. Depending on the project there may be a representative from worldwide marketing. During the proposal phases, representatives from service, manufacturing and quality development join the team. The core team is charged with the responsibility for guiding the project and making certain that the needs of respective departments are met. The team is the management of the project.

Marketing Manager, U S Electrical Engineering Company

We found several variants of the teamworking concept. Some teams are full-time, others are part-time. Some handle one, others handle several projects, depending on the complexity of the work in hand. In many firms, product change is such a fundamental part of the firm's operation that everyone is looking to become involved in product development work. In such an environment, teams emerge naturally and individuals are motivated to join them. In companies where teamworking is less likely to emerge as a natural response, the problem of implementing teamwork is tricky. Such companies may be rigidly organized along functional lines, and teams may need to be forced by top management. To be successful:

- Top management needs to recognize the need for product improvement teams and promote their credibility in the organization.
- Top management needs to identify potential team leaders and encourage them to take ownership of a project. Team leaders must shine in the role of organizers and must be able to gain the respect and commitment from their peers in other functions.
- Each functional head needs to respond by releasing members of his staff to participate in a team.

- Teams need to be allowed access to top management to help them progress projects.

All sorts of benefits can result from the establishment of product development teams. Cross-functional lines of communication are improved and functional specialists develop a better understanding of one another's jobs and skills. It is unlikely however, that introduction of the team concept alone will allow the firm to pursue product improvement adequately unless other factors in the 7S framework support it. In particular, teams need an explicit strategy to work to, from which top management derives checking measures to monitor progress. All in all, the team concept is only one key ingredient in the whole recipe for successful product improvement.

It has been argued that the necessary conditions for effective product improvement are an explicit strategy and an appropriate managerial style to generate shared commitment to development projects. These factors provide the right kind of climate in which multi-functional task groups or teams can operate effectively. In all these issues top management has a key role to play. However, these facts alone do not ensure success in product improvement activities. A team set up to carry out development work needs to be staffed with the right kind of managers and utilize skills appropriate to the work in hand. The team also needs to be guided by appropriate procedures and systems which ensure that developments are pursued thoroughly and are checked regularly. In short, staff, skills and systems, if handled appropriately, will allow teamwork to flourish.

Staffing product improvement teams

It has already been shown that staff engaged in product improvement can be at a low to middle management level. These managers are close to current operations and markets and can deal quickly and effectively with the nuts and bolts of product improvement. In high achieving firms, the issue of staffing the team is commonly taken a step further by explicitly considering the personal qualities looked for in managers participating in teams. These personal qualities focus on particular abilities and interpersonal skills.

Product improvement, no matter how minor, requires the interplay of the firm's many functional skills. It can become a highly complex process, both in terms of the development itself and in terms of seeking to adapt the firm's current operations to handle product improvement with the minimum cost and disruption. The wide array of factors that need to be taken into account prompt many firms to look for good organizers and administrators. In other words, people who are not only skilled in their own functional discipline, but are capable of managing their input in the context of the development as a whole. A major American manufacturer of electrical products commented that the approach of successful Japanese firms provides guidance for the qualities looked for:

The Japanese are very good administrators – that's good for product development, though not for invention. . . . To develop and launch modified products quickly is an administrative job.

Not only is the ability to organize and administer looked for, but appropriate interpersonal skills are needed. A team member who continues to operate in an 'over-the-wall' or 'not-invented-here' mode within the team, will undermine its cohesiveness. The type of persons looked for are those with the ability to rise above narrow functional interests and who can liaise effectively with others from very different managerial backgrounds. The importance of the personal qualities of the team and the way participants interact with each other is underlined by the fact that, in many high achieving firms, the appointed team leader nominates people he would like to work alongside him/her.

The qualities of the team leader himself are critically important. It was frequently pointed out to us in successful firms that the team leader is not viewed as a product champion in the traditional sense. As team manager, he is 'first among equals'. He calls the meetings and makes sure that the team's collective skills are fully utilized. This approach ensures that the whole team becomes the 'product champion':

The project leader has a special position in the team. He is not the boss. He must use his interpersonal skills to resolve disputes and negotiate stalemates. He has an obligation to seek the assistance of upper management if the project is suffering in any way he cannot remedy.

Marketing Manager, US Electronics Firm

The project manager is the person who shares his responsibility with the team and forces it to work together for the common good. He must lead because there is a natural tendency for individuals to remain loyal to their 'base' function.

Director, Departmental Plans, US Chemical Company

Skills for successful product improvement

The successful pursuit of product improvement requires, in a general sense, the skilled application of the firm's current operating strengths to modified conditions. Marketing and design skills are particularly valued in product improvement and it is to these two areas that we now turn.

Looking at the way firms that are successful at product improvement carry out their work, it becomes clear that these apply three key market-related skills:

- Product management
- Market analysis and segmentation
- Competitor analysis

In all high achiever businesses, the process of product management was clearly identifiable. This is not simply product management in the marketing sense of the word, where current products are monitored for profitability and supported by various advertising and promotional packages. What is employed in these firms is product management in a business sense whereby the broad product range is shaped and balanced to meet evolving market conditions. In some instances, product management was assigned to a single function. More often, however, it was carried out at a senior management level where product line decisions were considered in tandem with strategic business implications.

In stark contrast, many firms with a poor product improvement record had no recognizable system for managing current products:

85 per cent of our products are specially made for particular customers. So they are on the product range until a customer doesn't want them any more.

Marketing Manager, UK Paint Company

There are far too many products sold into too many markets. We don't know exactly what profits or losses we make from individual products – our costing system is not up to this.

Business Unit Manager, UK Mechanical Engineering Company

The reason why sound product management is so important is that the information generated from the product management process forms one of the key bases for formulating product development strategy. Aggressive product developers see product management as a key managerial job:

We're looking at a range of products and over a period of time you can see the profitability going down because of market pressures. We are already developing new products to replace these. The product life cycle had shortened considerably over the last two to three years.

Marketing Manager, US Food Products Company

Building on effective product management, high achieving companies apply the marketing skills of market analysis and segmentation to identify market opportunities and to generate ideas for product updates. These companies do not analyse markets using 'traditional' criteria, such as for instance in industrial markets, company size or industry type. They will seek to understand market structures and customer groupings using innovative segmentation techniques based on benefits sought, in-use behaviour and applications. Their detailed understanding of markets identifies market gaps and opportunities.

Given the importance of marketing skills, it was surprising how, in many of the less successful firms, particularly in the mechanical engineering sector, there is no formal marketing function. Often, in these circumstances, marketing is left to the head of the business.

One of the key sources of ideas for product improvement, as well as one of the key inputs into product development strategy, is an analysis of what competitors are doing. Competitor analysis involves proactive market monitoring, not simply briefing salesmen to report business lost to rivals:

The one thing that the Japanese do more than anything else is look at what the competition are coming up with. As soon as Canon launch on to the Japanese market we'll get details of that product immediately, and we can predict to within a month when that product will be launched into the UK market. .... All Japanese companies do this, and to a certain extent they cancel each other out. But they hammer Western competitors, who do this sort of competitor analysis hardly at all.

Marketing Manager, Office Products, Japanese Electronics Company

Market turbulence, in terms of driving the need for new product improvement, is often created, not by customers, but by competitors pursuing a strategy of gaining competitive advantage through product differentiation. For many high achieving firms, analysing what competitors are doing is as important as investigating at first hand customers' needs and preferences.

Systems

Having analysed the type of staff and skills that are necessary for successful product improvement, what kind of procedures or managerial systems should be employed to allow team members to work together effectively and quickly? Here we find one of the central dilemmas of the management of product change. In order to manage projects involving many people and many inputs there is a need to set up procedures and systems. However, these very systems can serve to stifle creativity and flexibility.

Systematic procedures are necessary

In firms with a less successful product improvement record, we frequently found that the product improvement process consists of a very simple three or four step procedure, as follows:

- Idea
- Technical development
- Testing with customers
- Launch

In many instances the product improvement process is not explicitly laid down. It simply evolves over time. Such an approach is seriously flawed. We frequently found that the question as to whether to proceed with a project would only be addressed formally early in the development process. But this is precisely when there is very little information about the project, particularly concerning its commercial viability. We found one firm which was rightly proud of the thoroughness of its screening procedures, but which was blissfully unaware that the value of these was negligible because screening was carried out very early in the process and not reviewed until the eve of launch:

Screening is a fairly involved process taking on many issues, including an assessment of business feasibility. Once we have conducted screening we have a 'live' brief which says: 'we'll end up with a product of this nature; in this price range; which will perform to these characteristics; in this marketplace; hence, we'll have this competitive edge.

Marketing Manager, UK Food Products Company

This is far too early in the process to assess all factors accurately. As a project progressed in the firm, there was no reassessment of viability, nor of changes in the external environment. Changing customer demands or competitor activity may render a project commercially unviable, requiring modified features or attributes which might make it a much better business proposition.

Lack of regular and continuous screening not only means that developments with a limited market potential absorb scarce resources, but also that project progress is not monitored. Regular checkpoints are needed to make sure the project is being driven according to an agreed time scale. The following comments made by managers in firms with poor product improvement records illustrate the issue:

I can think of a project on which we have been blowing hot and cold for about 14 years. We finally killed it off six months ago because we realized we were never going to get there efficiently.

Marketing Manager, US Mechanical Engineering Company

A lot of developments just trundle on. I call them bones – things you take out occasionally and just gnaw at. You don't really do anything with them, and then you put them back. We would be better eating the bone completely or not picking it up ever again.

Technical Manager, UK Mechanical Engineering Company

These examples illustrate that systems and procedures are required to ensure that product improvements capitalize on market opportunities and are monitored efficiently. Such systems need to enshrine the principle of multi-functional involvement to ensure all relevant issues are being addressed at each stage of the process and that information is fed back during all stages.

The companies we found that are high achievers in product improvement do have thorough and detailed procedures. In most cases these are written down in reference manuals which provide checklists. It was also noticeable that in all businesses intent on improving product development efforts, it was tighter and more institutionalized systems which were being focused on. Typically, in successful businesses, such procedures involved a seven to ten step process, each stage being characterized by informational inputs and development activities required, ending in a go/no go decision to be ratified by senior managers. The precise systems and process stages used are highly dependent on the firm concerned, but all embodied the following characteristics:

- Procedures used for the early stages are geared to ensuring that the development process itself generates information about the viability of the product concept in its market setting. For this purpose, a large amount of up-front exploratory work is encouraged.
- Once the product concept meets key criteria, procedures switch into a new mode designed to develop and implement the concept as quickly and efficiently as possible.
- Procedures allow for regular management checkpoints both to monitor project progress and re-evaluate the business worth of the improvement.
- Procedures enshrine multi-functional involvement. In this way each stage is not the responsibility of a single function, but requires the explicit involvement of all relevant functions.
- Procedures are updated regularly on the basis of experience of previous product improvement project work.

Allowing for flexibility

Systematic procedures are not, however, instant recipes for success. Some companies we visited that have recognized the need for thorough product improvement procedures and have instituted manuals and complex systems, experience difficulties in their operationalization. They find their control and co-ordination systems cumbersome to manage and are suspicious that these slow the development process. One marketing manager roundly condemned them because of their inability to discriminate between run-of-the-mill product improvements and potential high-fliers.

We believe that the key to understanding why some firms work well with complex systems, and others do not, lies in the nature of the task group being used. Firms that experience consistent difficulties with complex procedures often are those that assign different functions to oversee different stages. They do not use a single product development team. This in itself leads to delays and inhibits progress. Such firms, in our opinion, compound the problems of complex systems with a 'pass the parcel' approach to product development.

In high achiever firms we found the use of multi-functional teams counteracts the potential bureaucracy of complex procedures. The team can interpret the nature of the development reached so far and make an assessment of whether the next stage needs to be followed with more or less thoroughness. When this is done, the team can decide on the basis of its accumulated knowledge of the project whether to jump a particular stage, or whether to pursue some stages in parallel.

Moreover, changes occur all the time as a development progresses. Product improvement can often be unpredictable. The team must interpret whether changed information is valid input or not, and whether changes require an approach different from the standard one. It is in this way that companies that are more adept at product improvement cope with the tension between the need to formalize the process and the need to be flexible enough to react to ongoing changes in markets and in technology.

Conclusion

In this chapter we have shown how high achiever firms manage product improvement by means of the following.

- **An explicit strategy:** Product improvement efforts are underpinned by an explicit strategy, formulated by the heads of the firm's key functions and spearheaded by top management. Such detailed strategy provides the focus for idea generation in selected markets and helps to prioritize projects.
- **Sponsoring top management:** An explicit strategy enables top management to relinquish day-to-day control of particular projects. Instead, top management exerts control via the clear

strategic objectives against which progress is checked. Top management thereby becomes the sponsor of developments, unknotting any major problems

- **Shared ownership:** An explicit strategy and a supportive top management lays the groundwork for generating the shared values necessary to push development projects through operational hurdles.
- **Teamwork:** Teams of functional specialists are brought together to work on development projects. Such teamwork caters for the iterative and problem-solving process of product improvement, in which a whole series of options and solutions need to be discussed quickly.
- **Marketing and technical skill inputs:** Product improvement demands a detailed understanding of current markets to maximize synergies between existing and upgraded product offerings.
- **Systematic flexibility:** Procedures ensure that key issues are addressed formally during development, but nevertheless allow development teams the freedom to solve problems in their own way.

7

Effective New Product Development Practice

UPDATING and modifying current product offerings is only likely to sustain a firm's growth up to a certain point. The growing aggressiveness of competition in many markets means that opportunities for exploiting undeveloped market opportunities through product improvement are being reduced. Firms that rely solely on old products based on yesterday's technology risk being overtaken by competitors from both inside and outside their industries. Sooner or later, the firm will have to seek new growth. Firms that are the most vulnerable in this respect typically have the following characteristics:[1]

- They are usually large, old-established companies, and often describe themselves as the 'world's leading supplier' of a product.
- Their whole approach, as exemplified by their organizational structure, is product based.
- They have a massive investment in a manufacturing capability geared to low-cost production.
- They stick to the technology that they are leaders in, despite the fact that that technology may have been 'stretched' as far as possible.
- As a result of their large market share and cost-of-manufacture advantages, they make good short-term returns.
- They often perceive themselves to be leading product developers when in fact they are pursuing incremental product improvement in confined markets.

Strategic importance of new product development

Sheltering behind their massive market dominance, such firms are blissfully unaware that new technology may wipe out their position in an industry, or that other firms may be able to make more money as a result of pursuing imaginative new product development. The R&D director of a major American electronic instrument manufacturing firm felt, unlike his colleagues, that the company was on the brink of major problems:

Because we are making money, we are reluctant to change our strategy. There is a danger in only doing product improvement. More than 50 per cent of our products are now commodity products. I am worried that some new invention may well upset the total market structure.

The sweeping effects of technological change mean that new product development may be necessary not just for growth but for survival. Technological change is no respecter of industry boundaries. The microprocessor revolution has already demonstrated that major technological developments can affect industries from far outside the source of their traditional technology. In this way, electronic, electrical and mechanical technologies have effectively merged. This has resulted in major market restructuring, affecting the benefit packages sought by different markets.

The next generations of technological change – biotechnology and information processing – are likewise affecting a wide spread of industries. Biotechnology is an interesting example of how technological change can and will affect industries including those with an apparently low technological 'content' to their products. In this way, food manufacturing is likely to be revolutionized, along with pharmaceuticals, light chemicals and several other industrial sectors.

The implications are that leading players in an industry can no longer feel secure simply on the basis of their current technological know-how. They will have to scan a much wider technological, market and business horizon than ever before, and be prepared to develop new skills in pursuing business growth. In this way machine tool manufacturers have had to develop electronic engineering and software skills, as well as be ahead in mechanical engineering technology, to survive the market and technological turbulence that now affects them.

Developing new products and businesses to cope with radical technological and market change is not an easy option. Developing new products usually leads a firm into new business areas which are more risky. In contrast, the risks of product improvement are much less because, by and large, known markets are being dealt with, which makes the forecasting of sales much easier. The higher risks of new product development are compounded by the fact that new products usually only pay off in the longer term. These two factors make the idea of internal new product development an anathema to many firms. Also, shareholder pressure will often not tolerate a dip in profits to finance more radical and risky development work.

These factors make acquisition appear a very attractive route to securing footholds in new and potentially higher growth markets. A common perception is that acquisition is a quicker and cheaper method to grow than is internal product development:

At the moment we are at an unusual time in our history in the sense that we are losing our traditional business to competitors. So we are probably now more aggressive at funding new product opportunities than ever before. And these new opportunities, on the whole, are realized by acquisition. If we develop something on our own it takes 5–10 years. Right at the present I am not sure that we have 5–10 years.

Marketing Manager, US Mechanical Engineering Company

However, the companies we came across which solely pursue the acquisition route to growth are notably not the most successful. It is important to see that acquisition may not be the quick-fix remedy it appears to be. Acquisition has equally demanding skill requirements as internal new product development. Successfully merging different managerial and business skills is a rare art and also relies on much good fortune. Acquisition, moreover, may reduce the innovative capability of the organization as a whole. The creation of one large business can result in loss of small company atmosphere and in the variety of inputs which generate creativity. Moreover, opportunities for acquisition are reducing in many industrial sectors:

We have generally been a company which has grown through acquisition. The whole company was based on this. What has happened over time is that the opportunities to buy innovative small companies have diminished because so many people are now out there looking at this as a way to grow.

Marketing Manager, US Food Products Company

New product development is, in fact, a very useful route to growth. It can be made into a cost-effective and attractive route by the careful management of risks and costs. Firms that are high achievers in new product development deal head-on with the risks and costs by carefully developing a strategy for new product development based on the company's inherent strengths. The new product development process is then consciously managed to reduce costs and risks to acceptable levels.

Managing new product development using the 7S framework

The characteristics of new product development, particularly the inherent risks, demand a different managerial approach. Once more, we find the McKinsey framework useful for diagnosing the way firms can best manage this complex task.[2] Box 7.1 summarizes, under each of the 7S headings, the factors which characterize the managerial approach adopted by firms that are high achievers in new product development. It will be noted that the application of

Box 7.1   Key factors in managing new product developments successfully

---

Top management's direct responsibilities

- **Strategy:** Formulated on the basis of the company's core strengths.
- **Style:*** Top management needs to be directly involved and to take the lead.
- **Shared values:*** There needs to be a shared understanding of the necessity for new product developments.
- **Structure of task group:** High level 'agents of change' separated from the mainstream organization to progress new product projects.

Teamwork aspects

- **Staff:** Staff involved need to have 'intrapreneurial' abilities, acting as mini-businessmen within the organization.
- **Skills:** An ability to interpret macro changes in the market and technical environment and to relate these to the firm's core strengths.
- **Systems:** Innovative systems need to be devised to reduce development hurdles and risks.

---

* Shared values and management style appear under the remit of top management. While the effects of these two factors manifest themselves in teamworking, they result from top management's actions.

the 7Ss to the task of new product development is markedly different from that for product improvement. For example, top management is directly involved in a hands-on way in new product development projects, and the task group is separated off from the mainstream organization.

Ideally, for new product development, the 7Ss will work in a way which frees up the organization to think more creatively about the need for long-term growth. In terms of implementing particular projects, the 7Ss need to be operationalized in a way which allows the firm to pursue projects that are less constrained by the demands of current business operations. The retention of direct control by top management ensures that such freedom does not result in proposals which are incapable of being implemented, or which lead the business into areas that are incompatible with the overall strategy.

The factors are again analysed in turn, looking first at those that are influenced by and involve top management directly. In this chapter there is less reference to firms that have a poor new product development record. The reason for this is that firms in the sample for which new product development is not a major contributor to sales growth either concentrate efforts on product improvement, or attempt to handle the new product development task in the same way as updated or modified products. However, as we shall show, the task of new product development requires a quite different managerial approach. The analysis is again illustrated with extensive quotations.

Top management's role

The strategy, managerial style and structure of the task group appropriate for new product development is dealt with first. This is because top management has a key role to play in ordering all these factors and is instrumental in recognizing that the new product development task demands a special managerial approach. The actions and behaviour of top management can ensure that new product development efforts are actively pursued within an organization and appropriately supported. This is important because top management has to become much more proactively involved in the pursuit of new product developments. It is a high-risk high-cost activity which cannot be left to the inventiveness and personal endeavours of middle and lower management.

A loose-tight strategy for new product development

Because radical product development is expensive and discontinuous, it needs to be recognized explicitly within the overall corporate strategy. Without formal recognition, investment is unlikely to be earmarked for new developments and no developments of any consequence are likely to take place, even when a firm stumbles by chance on a good business opportunity. It is in the area of strategy for new product development that we encounter yet another dilemma in the management of product change.

Many firms contend that, beyond the basic allocation of research expenditure, one cannot have a strategy for new products because, by definition, one does not know what opportunities are going to appear on the horizon. Firms that adopt this kind of 'non-strategic' approach to new product development frequently have a lot of money invested in corporate research laboratories or in think-tanks and leave to fate what next product innovation will emerge from their creative hot-beds. Under this system, it is very difficult to assess the value and cost benefit of research monies. Moreover, in them, research bodies will often go off into 'blue skies' research, and it is left to chance whether the resultant new product concepts will be of much commercial use. Indeed, it is frequently the case that such firms end up with a technological solution looking for a problem.

Focusing efforts

With this type of speculative approach to new product development, there is very little control over the two factors which need close control: risks and costs. By not defining what is wanted from new product development research efforts, the firm can never be sure that an investment is worthwhile. This leads to reticence over continued funding, and frequently in such firms R&D expenditure is the first on the list of candidates to be reduced in times of trouble. In contrast, firms skilled at new product development regularly underpin research activities with a strategy:

We need to direct our research ... we don't want to wait for a new development to come along and say: 'Eureka! – this is going to take us into the so-and-so business ...'. We need to provide a focus for research which will take us into the areas we want to go.

Division Head, U K Agro-Chemicals Company

It is a matter of approach. We believe we must start looking for business opportunities out there in the marketplace, not by encouraging brilliant inventions and then looking for applications.

V-P Technology, US White Goods Manufacturer

As with product improvement, it is the way strategy is formulated, rather than its precise content, which will provide most guidance to firms that wish to pursue new product development effectively. The success of firms in pursuing new product development is often based on the way strategy is implemented. Successful firms devise a strategy that can be described as simultaneously loose-tight. The tightness comes from what might be called 'anchor points' in the strategy. Such anchor points are found by answering three basic questions:

- In what ways can we capitalize on core strengths?
- How can our core strengths be enhanced and developed?
- What are the key dimensions and trends affecting the evolution of market needs?

The answers to these questions define the strategic arena within which the firm can map out the most effective growth routes for new product development and will provide the rationale and focus for research efforts.

Assessing strengths

Looseness in the strategy comes from the way the questions are answered. In many firms, the temptation is to answer the questions in terms of the way current strengths and markets are defined. However, successful firms think about these questions laterally. They ask themselves how they could use current assets in a different way, and what strengths could potentially be developed from the existing base. Companies that are good at devising strategies for new product development will look at their strengths in the widest sense. Breadth of vision comes from the following:

- Taking into account the entire value chain: research, marketing, operations, distribution, suppliers, etc.
- An ability to see how those strengths can be used in new ways.
- An astute assessment of how inherent strengths can be built on and modified to develop new competences in new areas.

A newly appointed development director of a US food company demonstrated how looking at the organization from a different angle can generate new product opportunities:

When I took this job it struck me that we had the potential to grow organically. It struck me that there were strengths which had not been fully utilized. Like our size. Like our 2000 sales people. So I considered that we should be able to develop some new products which would use these existing resources.

A marketing manager in an American company manufacturing consumer electrical products pointed out that it was prepared to undertake any type of new product development as long as it built on existing strengths in the value chain:

Yes, we do constrain ourselves. We will not go chasing any diversification opportunity – there must be a strategic basis for success as far as one of our key capabilities is concerned. We have assessed each of these elements in the value chain in relation to the competition. So, to repeat, there must be some basis for anticipating success based on existing strengths .... I am looking for product solutions to market needs. The challenge is to take technology and combine it with our market and distribution strengths to give the consumer something he needs. The trick is to supply that need in a way which is better than in the past.

This company recognizes that key capabilities are derived from each element of the value chain, and accordingly views technical strengths, manufacturing capabilities, marketing strengths, sales and distribution skills and after-sales service as factors to be capitalized on in new product development.

Assessing market needs

An analysis of strengths needs to be married with an assessment of the evolving marketplace. Many businesses attempt to assess developing market needs only by monitoring the performance of current products. Such a product-based approach blinds the company to wider developments:

Our competitors see the market growing very slowly ... they are looking for steady growth from traditional product lines. But we have never been committed solely to the industry we are currently in. Our commitment has been to meeting customers needs.

Managing Director, U K Packaging Company

Firms need to step back from their current market conditions, to understand the basic nature of customer needs and wider technological or lifestyle developments which may affect those needs and lead to the emergence of new types of consumer demand. One of the ways of doing this is to define customer needs in the widest possible terms:

New product development in this company is designed to grow the company. We define our business as earth-moving, not in product terms. We are not in fork-lift trucks, crawlers, excavators, loading shovels, we are in earth-moving. We have to stay alive to the possibility that someone from another industry might come along and offer a facility for digging holes. It is not always easy, but it helps to look at the market in broader terms.

Technical Director, U K Construction Equipment Company

Defining the business mission in the widest possible sense helps the firm to recognize the wider potential markets open to it. It also allows it to be alive to the many industries and technologies that may provide substitute products and therefore pose serious competitive threats. Most high achiever businesses display this non-conservative approach. In this way, for example, a food manufacturer whose current product range is in snacks and crisps will consider itself to be in the 'casual eating' business.

Recognizing changing lifestyle patterns is a fundamental starting point for assessing new product opportunities in consumer industries. For instance, air conditioning was available in houses and offices long before it was available in cars, but the need was there all the time. It needed someone to interpret the need as a business proposition. The growth of working women has encouraged the trend for convenience eating, which in turn has affected meal preparation. These trends have given rise to opportunities for food manufacturers to produce complete meal ranges and for consumer durable producers to develop microwave cookers and other cooking aids.

Assessing these kinds of trends requires a company to stand back from its current activities and to interpret the nature of consumer and industrial markets in the widest possible sense. It requires a 'whither the world?' type of approach, in which all kinds of trends are encompassed and assessed for their effects on future markets.

Putting strengths and needs together

We found several examples of companies that consciously develop a strategy for their new product development effort by combining an understanding of long-term marketplace changes with an interpretation of their own strengths. For illustration purposes, two companies from very different industries will be focused on.

In a major American chemical company, we found that every three years, a complete analysis is made of potential technological and market developments over the next decade. This is an explicit and wide-ranging exercise involving the company's planning function and internal and external experts on markets and technologies. The description of the process, given by the planning director, demonstrates the company's astute application of its own strengths to evolving market needs:

What we did was to assess our present strengths and to project the link between markets and technology in the future. What we did was to take each one of the new markets we identified and develop a grid showing what each will be worth to us by the year 2000 assuming different levels of capability on our part.

The starting point of the assessment was the question: 'Where are we presently in the areas that are going to be significantly bigger by the year 2000?' Further: 'If we ride the horses that we are on now, where will they take us?' In the automobile industry for instance, we are working on replacing sheet metal for bodies. In the future this will be a very competitive environment. We calculated a probability range of where our competitors are going to be. From the distillation of these assessments we decided to concentrate on areas of new emerging technology which would allow us access into new growth markets. Without going into details, I can tell you that some of these are going to be very different from our traditional business activities.

Through this careful process, the firm has been able to target its research and so plan to develop the technology it needs to access new business areas. In a very different industry, food manufacturing, we found another US company developing its strategy using the same basic approach:

We did not start with new product ideas. I started with my definition of what I thought the company had as its strengths and I used that to say: 'given these strengths, let us talk to customers about their needs, wants and opportunities and see how they fit in with our strengths'. You could go the other way round and say, look at all the opportunities .... What I did, however, was constrain our thoughts by considering the strengths of the company and how we deliver versus consumer needs. This process identified a set of new product opportunities for us.

In this company it is the Vice-President responsible for strategy and development who is the key focal point in this process. He draws in other functional specialists – internal and also external – to help him put the strategy together. As long as the new product opportunities capitalize on the strengths of the company, any type of new development is considered. The strategic horizon used is five years, updated every six months. Significantly, it was felt that the rigour of the strategy setting process in this company had reduced resistance to innovation:

By very carefully analysing the market needs – particularly over long future time spans, we have been able to make top management more comfortable about releasing the large sums of money needed for new product projects.

Both these examples are from companies that had in the past dragged their feet in terms of new product development. Now recognizing that their traditional markets and ways of operating would not sustain continued growth, they consciously took a step back from current activities to look to the future. Significantly, they are prepared to use external consultants as catalysts in developing a new view of their opportunities.

These examples also clearly illustrate a loose-tightness in strategy formulation which allows a firm to think creatively about the future without going into areas where none of its 'distinctive competences' are capitalized on:

The key for successful new product development is to start from someplace where you have strengths or which you at least understand.

Marketing Manager, US Food Products Company

This approach maps out the strategic ground between what some analysts call 'sticking to the knitting', which implies too much conservatism in product development, and unrestrained diversification, in which the firm's inherent strengths are not applied to temper the risks and costs involved in new product development. Moreover, this type of strategic approach to new product development generates a whole series of new business opportunities. The process does not begin with a focus on products, current or anticipated, but begins with a total market view. It is that market view, overlaid with a creative assessment of the firm's current and latent strengths, which will show up areas that can feasibly be exploited with new products.

Management style

When looking at the role top management plays in new product development, again the twin issues of risk and cost emerge. Because new product development is high risk and high cost, top management needs to take a much greater leadership role than in product improvement. In companies successful at new product development, top management does not merely support the firm's efforts in this area, but actually leads the process. Ideally, the new product development effort is headed by a director (or vice-president) who can represent interests at board level. New product developments require this high visibility in order to ensure the resources and support are made available.

Top management activity in new product development operates on two levels. First there is a need to communicate an understanding of developments that are being undertaken to secure the company's future. We found several instances of CEOs regularly touring company offices to explain their board's vision of the company's future. At the second level, the top manager heading the firm's new product development effort needs to see himself both in the role of a senior manager, having the power and authority to facilitate the work, and in the role of a business team manager, working with a group of managers in a highly participative way:

I do play a co-ordinating role in the sense that there are certain things where you need someone with my title to get involved to push things along .... I try and make this clear to everyone who works with me ... down to the most junior person who comes and talks with me.

V-P Strategy & Development, US Food Products Company

Whereas the role of top management in product improvement centres on sponsorship and facilitation, in new product development, top management has to directly drive development projects. Extra leverage is required to push along what are inherently risky developments. Moreover, because new projects often involve making unprecedented decisions, established procedural control is usually incapable of providing the necessary guidance. Top management, therefore, has to be close enough to the project, and involved directly in its evolution to make sound decisions. Using Tushman and Nadler's terms, this is where top management 'envision, energize and enable' the new product development program.[3] The precise nature of top management's role in this task will become apparent in the discussion on staffing.

Shared understanding

Unlike product improvement, where everyone is likely to be involved in or directly affected by the process, new product development demands that a separate group be commissioned to pursue tasks outside the mainstream organization. This presents problems for instilling necessary commitment to new product development work from the whole organization. Separation can often lead to exclusivism and feelings of distrust. We were told of cases where the legs of the new product development task group had been cut off by the mainstream organization, worried that its future was in jeopardy from new developments.

Mavericks or 'accepted intrapreneurs'?

Because of the dilemma between needing a separate unit to undertake new product development and the need for the total organization to be committed to the future, we found instances where new product development agents within an organization act as mavericks. They have the ear of the board, but act in great secrecy with respect to the rest of the organization. However, given the fact that new product developers need to draw on the strengths of the total organization and manipulate these in new ways, this approach is always likely to be limiting.

In other firms we found the new product developers themselves working hard to develop an understanding within the mainstream organization of their purpose. Through efforts at 'internal marketing' new product developers become 'accepted intrapreneurs':

We have used our work as a method of raising morale within the division as a whole. To show people that we are going for new opportunities for everyone.

Director, New Products/New Markets, U S Consumer Electronics Company

The importance of generating a shared understanding of the need for new product development efforts at all levels within the organization cannot be underestimated. In the case of product improvement, the necessity for updating and modifying current products is more likely to be understood and not seen as undermining the security of the current operation and jobs within it. In new product development, however, the potential for the mainstream organization to feel threatened is considerable. Resistance to radical change can dramatically affect the ability of the new product development team to operate effectively and to utilize the inherent strengths of the total organization. Preventing such resistance is a top management task which requires sensitivity and perception.

Structuring task groups

We found that firms that are successfully engaging in new product development set up separate organizational units, outside the mainstream organization, dedicated to handling new projects. In this way, new product developments are considered as a supra-divisional activity. There is a clear rationale for splitting off the management of new product development from the management of the existing business (including product improvement). The systems used to manage an established stable business can easily stifle embryonic developments. Established businesses are by and large revenue generators, whereas new areas under development are cost centres.

Separating out these two areas organizationally allows for the application of different managerial systems and performance measures.

Putting new development work within the established business risks that traditional management approaches will almost certainly be applied. Such methods are likely to be incompatible with the need to develop something new and innovative:

> By putting these developments in the established organization, they would be smothered, or would be so encumbered by the established way of doing things that you would find it very difficult to do the things you need to.

> *Planning Director, UK Electronics Company*

The separation of the work organizationally from the existing business serves to underline that a totally new approach is needed. People staffing these units become aware that they need to adopt perspectives outside the current business operation in order to assess broad technological and other opportunities:

> It does not make sense to put these new developments within our traditional business. You see, it is essential to focus on the ongoing business. New product business has to be handled with care. Our sort of new product ideas are more speculative – different animals, so we said: 'let's put different sorts of people on them'. That's why a different organization was set up under me to do just that.

> *V-P Strategy & Development, US Food Products Company*

A separate unit to handle new product developments is also necessary to cope full-time with the inevitable complexity and costs involved. Companies that are struggling with new product development usually call on the existing organization to carry out this work. Inevitably, under this system persons do not have enough time to spend on projects because day-to-day issues take over:

> We have decided to develop our new telephone equipment outside the company making that equipment, even though part of the development may end up there. This is partly to overcome the inertia which stems from (i) the lack of technical know-how and (ii) the fact that they are too busy with the existing business.

> *Technical Director, UK Electronics Company*

Apart from separation from the mainstream organization, the other characteristic of new product units is that they are placed at a high level within the organization, headed usually by a director or vice-president. This is of vital importance. More seniority is required to promote and manage complex, costly and important new product development activities. The high visibility and profile of these groups helps them to attract the resources needed to carry out their work.

We have found that two main ways are used organizationally to split new product development work from other activities. One is to use a separate body as an agent of change, working up concepts that will then be grafted on in some way to the mainstream organization. The other is to set up a skeletal business unit which will eventually blossom into a fully-fledged part of the organization running its own business. We look at these two mechanisms in turn.

New product development units as 'agents of change'

Many high technology companies that set up separate units as agents of change within the organization use what is sometimes referred to as the 'sponsored research lab' approach. In these circumstances, existing business units may sponsor central research laboratory work to carry out radical developments:

Our business units are levied a percentage of turnover which goes into the Central Research Fund (CRF). Say a business puts in £2m, then it will want to suggest a project on which the £2m or more can be spent. The CRF system ensures that there are proper commercial objectives for all development work, otherwise you get into the blue skies area. Our two corporate research labs can produce prototypes and even simulate small-scale batch production, but we would want this to be clearly sponsored by a business.

Technical Director, UK Electronics Company

The sponsored approach has developed from a disenchantment with the ability of corporate research laboratories to create new product ideas independently of business units. However, any sponsored approach has to be well managed. Asking technical research groups to come up with new developments assumes that technology is the most appropriate strength to build on. While research laboratories will undoubtedly produce new product concepts, they will rarely have the tools or skills to consider these in the context of a total business proposition. Moreover, sponsorship by existing businesses means that they will mostly be looking for new ideas in the context of their current business operation. So instead of separating off the new product development work in order to develop a new approach to business opportunities, what many of these companies have effectively done is to make sure that their central research work is managed more closely.

Another example of the 'agent of change' approach is afforded by companies that set up multi-functional 'think tanks' to conceptualize new business opportunities. These groups of people, drawn from several functions, are charged with thinking about the future in markets delineated by the new product development strategy setting process. In one company we found the use of 'innovation cells' to do this:

The whole purpose of the innovation cells is to release people from their tight functional responsibilities to address new tasks and opportunities for the long run.... To look at opportunities that might otherwise not be seen to fit into our existing strengths in a conventional sense.

Marketing Manager, U S White Goods Manufacturer

Such units are charged with identifying new product opportunities and typically have a budget to carry out initial development work. After the concept has been worked up into a tangible product, developments are handed back to the mainstream organization. Similarly, in another American company, we found a Director of New Products/New Markets whose job it is to 'sell new ideas to the organization'. He sets up task forces drawn from the existing structure to help him investigate various aspects of a business opportunity. He sees his role to start up projects, to do the early development work, and then to hand over to an established business unit.

These 'agents of change' are certainly useful for identifying new opportunities that otherwise would not have been picked up in the course of the ongoing business. However, the problems of grafting on new developments to the mainstream organization cannot be underestimated. Successful new product developments do not just involve a new piece of product hardware. A whole new business concept may be required involving different distribution, manufacturing and marketing systems. The current organization, the way it is set up and managed may not be able to cope with this:

We don't have many examples of where we have been successful at grafting an innovative development on to the ongoing business. It's something we are concentrating on at the moment.

Technical Director, U K Electronics Company

All the examples quoted above come from firms that had fairly recently realized that new product development requires a different managerial approach. In meeting the challenge by setting up units which provide the catalyst for change, they have only effectively dealt with the initiation of new product ideas. Successful new product development, however, requires the management of implementation as well as initiation. We anticipate that these firms will move to using skeletal business teams to handle new projects right the way through the development process as they begin to realize that new ideas are not being fully capitalized on because of handover problems.

New product development units as skeletal businesses

We have found that a potentially more effective approach is to set up the team charged with new product development as a full-time skeletal business unit. In this, a group of functional specialists is brought together headed by someone who is, in essence, a business manager. Business teams are like mini-venture groups, but with a more focused vision. Unlike the free-wheeling venture groups of the past, skeletal business teams have specific objectives. New product development opportunities have already been identified by the strategy setting process masterminded by top management. The team is thereafter charged with developing particular offering packages. The value of this approach lies in the fact that, by being structured as an embryonic business unit, the team strives to develop not just a piece of product hardware, but a total business proposition.

There are no handover problems, because once the new concept is developed, there is a ready-made team to manage it into commercialization. In other words, the team ultimately becomes a fully fledged strategic business unit within the mainstream organization. Not only is this a more logical approach to new product development, but the fact that the team is made up of potential managers for the new business inspires and motivates considerably. It also ensures thoroughness: if the team inadequately thinks through an aspect of the development, it has to live with that decision when it becomes exposed to running the business in real life. We now show the way two companies use skeletal business teams to carry out new product development:

In a large American chemical company two variants of the skeletal business team approach are currently used. In cases where a new product development is conceptually compatible with a current business, the new product team is 'piggybacked' on to an existing business unit:

These new product units are cost centers not revenue generators, so we keep them separated. We talk about core businesses and new initiatives. Initiatives that directly support existing businesses are managed within established strategic business units.

The basic advantage of this approach is that 'initiatives' can be nurtured under the umbrella of an existing strategic business unit. The initiative does not have to bear the total burden of the resources needed to develop the new business as it can draw on the resources and skills of the established business.

However, the company recognizes that there are problems with 'piggybacking', because established businesses are inherently resistant to absorbing a drain on their resources:

The real problem is that when you do piggybacking with an established product group, they may not want to do it because they don't want to absorb some of the losses. This is when you need a Group Vice-President who says: 'you will do it', and gives them some exemptions in terms of performance accounting.

For new initiatives which do not fit easily into the current operation, the company adopts a different approach. For this purpose, multi-functional business teams are set up outside the mainstream organization:

Here we are dealing with initiatives which are unsponsored. They are initiatives that are not obviously or intimately tied up with any existing business unit, but which fall within the umbrella of our whole business. These are managed outside established strategic business units.

Such teams are 'housed' in the R&D Department with the director acting as sponsor:

We have recently created a 'hatchery' which is nominally housed in R&D but really has a business charter. We've organized this hatchery as a collection of new business teams. The teams are multi-functional – each team has responsibility for market development, manufacturing process development, as well as technical development .... Each is headed by a single entrepreneurial leader and his responsibility is literally to create the whole business. He has a mandate to make deals with potential partners including customers.

It is important to emphasize that these teams have direct access to top management. They live in a flat organization which allows them to function effectively:

We've put these teams together so that there is no formal organization other than the Development Director and the team. There is no hierarchy of people with split responsibility. So far it seems manageable, and it seems to allow the team leader enough head to do the kind of things he needs to do.

R&D Director, US Chemical Company

By setting up teams to manage new product development, either on the back of an existing strategic business unit or within the R&D 'hatchery', this company has found that the whole process of new product development is speeded up. Teams rapidly become exposed to solving real problems: their only *raison d'être* being the success of the new development:

We have found that the concept of teams is useful in situations of enormous technical complexity and high uncertainty. Teams find ways of solving things quickly. If we'd approached it in the traditional way, it would have taken twice as long. The team is in the situation of having to get round barriers – it can't hang around.

In another large US company, this time in food manufacturing, we found another variant of the skeletal business team concept at work. Unlike the above example, this company is functionally organized, yet still manages to use the business team concept. For this purpose a new division was recently set up under a Vice-President for Strategy and Development. Under him, self-standing business teams have been established to explore new business opportunities. Although the division is staffed mainly by ex-marketeers, the teams are charged with developing all aspects of a business proposition: manufacturing, production, design, as well as marketing. To do this, teams draw on extra skills to be found both inside and outside the mainstream organization. Members of skeletal business teams are motivated by the knowledge that once a development has reached the point of commercialization, it will be the team members who become the managers of the new business.

The examples above demonstrate that firms that have set up supra-divisional think-tanks to identify new opportunities in an effort to loosen up their organization have not gone far enough. Such agents of change are simply charged with suggesting new product opportunities with the initiatives being passed back to the mainstream organization for proper development. Major new developments will often require quite new delivery systems which cannot be supplied by the mainstream organization. To engage successfully in major new product development requires a sheltered organizational unit to be created. But the unit should not be sheltered from strategic objectives, for it needs to work on identified business opportunities which are seen as being acceptable to the corporation of which it hopes to become an established part.

Teamworking

So far it has been shown that the necessary conditions for effective new product development consist of:

- An appropriate loose-tight strategy which identifies the strategic arena for new business opportunities.
- Top management leadership and the inculcation of shared understanding of the necessity for new product development.
- A specially commissioned organizational unit, separated off from the mainstream organization, to progress development.

These factors lay the groundwork for new product development but do not, of themselves, assure success. The team charged with progressing developments must also be staffed appropriately, and must be guided by procedures and systems which do not suppress creativity. It is to factors that come under the heading of teamworking, that we turn now.

Staffing new product development cells

The staff required for new product developments is different from staff needed for product improvement projects. Senior managers in high achieving firms consistently cited three qualities looked for when deciding who should staff new product development teams:

- Ability to envision a new business operation.
- Ability to work in an unstructured and uncertain environment.
- Ability to implement, not simply design, a new business.

Effective new product development requires staff to act as 'mini' business managers. These managers need to have the capability to step outside a functional psyche and the traditions of current business operations. The Vice-President Strategy and Development in an American food manufacturer summed up these requirements as follows:

I need people who don't operate in quite the same way they would on an established brand – it's not a different type of person – it's just getting them to try and think more broadly. They have to be business people, not marketeers or technologists – they have to think about everything.

In contrast a Technical Director of a British electronics company lamented the lack of such qualities in the staff available to him:

There is an inability to see bigger trends – an inability to spot the possibility that we may not have telephones in the future. The convergence of computing and telecommunications presents enormous opportunities for new business development, but only a few persons can see these and act on their vision.

Not only do the staff of new product development units have to be capable of envisioning a new business operation by rising above their past experiences in the mainstream organization, they also have to be capable of working inside an unstructured and uncertain environment. The risk of new product development and the decisions that have to be made during the course of the development process make the task singularly difficult in terms of judging progress and achievement. Many projects fall by the wayside, and such 'failures' have the potential for demotivating and discouraging staff. Not all types of manager feel comfortable working in such circumstances.

The staff appropriate for new product development clearly need to have the ability to implement the new business vision. They need to translate an opportunity into concrete reality. This requires them to find new and innovative ways, which may be very different from traditional ways of working, to get a project off the ground. In short, they also need the qualities of 'fixers' – people who can find ways over development hurdles and deal with all aspects of a business proposition:

I've got people who would, in the established organization conceivably have never been inside a manufacturing plant – and now they're designing plant with the help of contractors.

V-P Strategy & Development, U S Food Products Company

The qualities described above will help to ensure that uncertain and high risk developments do not fail simply because the staff pursuing them are incapable of handling the managerial conditions. As in the case of product improvement, the qualities of the leader of a new product team are of vital importance. We found that in high achiever firms a senior manager is chosen who is considered to be an in-company entrepreneur, or 'intrapreneur'. Such a manager will frequently have proved himself previously in line or general management.

Skills

The successful pursuit of new product development requires appropriate skills to initiate developments and implement them. Initiation skills can be described, in a general sense, as 'helicopter factors'. They involve a firm rising above its current operations and markets to develop a new vision of the future. Unlike product improvement, it is important to understand that traditional marketing skills are of only limited use when trying to identify and conceptualize future business opportunities. Marketing tools, such as market research, only work fully when an existing market is fairly clearly defined.

Successful new product developer firms are characterized by neither being technology nor marketing-led in their approach to new product development. Potential new product ideas, originating in the technical skill base of the firm, are fused with marketing input to ensure a 'need-pull' for the new product. Conversely, feedback from the marketplace is carefully related to existing and future technological developments to ensure that the most up-to-date technological solutions are applied. Importantly, these firms aim to have technical and marketing skill bases of equal sophistication. Skills are applied in assessing the three related environments which provide the focus for generating new product opportunities: the market environment, the internal environment, and the technological environment.

In terms of implementation, we found high achiever firms less able to single out particular skills that they felt were prerequisites for successful new product development. In their responses to our questions, it became clear that projects pursued under the umbrella of new product development are diverse and situation specific, meaning that common skill requirements were difficult to distill. What appears crucial, however, is the qualities of the staff involved. These are considered the primary skill base from which projects, which by their nature are radically new, can be handled effectively. Within this context, skills in risk assessment were highlighted by the Vice-President Strategy and Development in one of our high achieving American firms as being particularly important:

I get nervous about the word entrepreneur because that implies risk-taking. I don't want people who are crazy risk-takers. What I want are persons who are extremely good at risk-assessment, which I consider is very different. They understand the cost of the risk and the upside of what it would be if it pays off. To me that is one of the key skills because everything is risky. I want people who understand enough about what they're doing to weigh the balance of the risk. That's what I call risk-assessment.

Partnering

The factors that cause the process of new product development to be costly and risky principally concern the need to develop new skills to handle new product concepts. In high achieving firms, this issue has been handled in a variety of ways. Instead of spending a great deal of money trying to develop these new skills afresh, the team set up as a skeletal business acts as an entrepreneur and looks around the internal and external communities for needed skills. In this connection the concept of 'partnering' is potentially valuable:

We also have the concept of external partnerships; that is to say, partnering with people to help drive the definition process; the development, and also commercialization. Historically, we would have thought we had to do it all on our own. However, we have found that the shortest route to commercialization is often through a customer who joins us in the development to help us find the answers.

R&D Development Director, US Chemical Company

When I was a brand manager I had to stick to the rules we had. Now I am learning to break the rules in the interest of speedy development. I don't automatically think of making a new product on our existing plant. We may not even use our own R&D people – we may use consultants. These are all things you don't consider when modifying products.

New Business Manager, US Food Products Company

It is important to see that the idea of partnering is explored in relation to every link in the value chain. In this way partnerships in development, distribution, manufacturing and marketing are all considered. It is also important to see that partnerships can be created with units in the existing organization. Indeed, these internal partnerships are needed for the company to capitalize on its existing strengths. We found a new product development unit which actively negotiates with the organization's mainstream distribution arm to set up a new system for their handling of new developments:

Previously another part of this company would have gone out and bought a lot of trucks to handle the distribution of this new development. I considered other parts of the company's organization and looked for things we could do with their systems for this project. In this way we avoided great costs.

Manufacturing partnerships are especially important. In large well-established businesses the manufacturing capability will be almost solely geared to low cost production. This can make the manufacturing arm of a company inflexible and unresponsive to the demands of new products. Many Western companies are only just beginning to realize the advantages of sub-contracting in making them more responsive and flexible to changing product offerings. Successful Japanese companies in contrast are often 'hollow' corporations using their sub-contracting arrangements to allow them to chop and change product ranges quickly. The companies we found to be the most successful at new product development regularly consider manufacturing partnerships as a possible route to progressing a new product development quickly.

New approaches to market testing

The other development task which successful new product developers play close attention to is testing the new product concept. Product testing is considered vital, not principally to test whether the product works, but to gather hard information about the total business concept. It is interesting to note that successful companies are not reticent about going to selected customers with a half-finished concept. They will use marketplace feedback to help them complete the conceptual design, and gain more insight into how the product can be positioned and marketed.

In industrial companies, early prototypes are worked up as quickly as possible and sent out for 'interactive' testing with potential users:

Traditional market research people are very good at telling you what's happening right now, but if you're really dealing with truly innovative products which end up in usages which are hard to envisage, this is no use. So we've been doing things like getting standard prototype products out into the field to begin to get hard insight into what the market potential is, and to recognize that this company isn't smart enough to produce the exact product entirely the way the market wants it. So before we invest an enormous amount of development money we will know approximately what type of product we're going to sell, who's going to buy it, and what its going to sell for. So the uncertainty is reduced before we commit major capital resources.

R&D Director, US Chemical Company

In the food industry, test marketing has fallen from favour because of the massive amounts of money involved, and reluctance by the trade to accept product tests. However, successful product developers in this industry do not shy away from testing products in innovative ways to obtain market feedback. These methods are not for the purists. They are quick and dirty but effective:

We view ourselves as trying to create test tube successes rather than gallon jug successes. Typically, tests in the established organization would involve 4–6 markets and a lot of money. In my tests we can go into 17 stores in a concentrated way because I can learn a lot of things from this and this minimizes the risk in both financial terms and in terms of success. I can predict success from results from these 17 stores. It may not be totally quantifiable – but qualitatively I'll know.

Marketing Manager, U S Food Products Company

In high achieving firms, testing the product concept in key market areas is not primarily driven by the need to verify the functional acceptance of the product hardware. It is specifically designed to generate more information about the business proposition as a whole, so reducing the overall risk involved in commercialization.

Systems

The above examples illustrate that firms pursuing new product development are willing to use different methods and techniques at different stages to address key tasks in the development process. Accordingly, the systems and procedures employed are characterized by being loose. This looseness comes from the recognition that a new business concept, by definition, will need to be developed in totally new ways. The skeletal business team is therefore given a great deal of latitude in how to progress:

What we are trying to do is a better and better job of moving from invention, where there's no clear developed market need, to a proven prototype in the market. So we try and create a separate atmosphere for these fledgling businesses wherein they can go out and get the process of iteration going in the marketplace and get a prototype made. We want to encourage our people to explore what kind of business it might be without forcing and choking it into a mould.

R&D Development Director, U S Chemical Company

In as far as this loose system can be characterized, the first stages of the process involve the business team working out how to progress development. The team discusses with top management whether partnerships within or outside the business are needed, whether patents are required, and what type of milestones should be set up to monitor the new development. Unlike product improvement, where prior experience already determines the nature of the process and the time scales required, the new product development team deliberately starts from a zero-base situation. Once an initial debate has taken place, the team sets about doing early development work.

This usually involves getting prototypes to key market groups to generate the information needed to develop a better definition of the whole potential business concept. Once information has been collected from customer interaction, a clearer business definition is drawn up outlining what must be done:

It's only at this stage that you can make an intelligent decision to kill the thing. You can't do a paper exercise until you have hard feedback from the marketplace.

R&D Director, US Chemical Company

Until this point top management will have deliberately shielded the new development from hard business questions, allowing the team to work out its own definition of what business opportunity it is working with. From this point on, the development process takes a more traditional format. The team is exposed to more and more rigorous reviews, the nature of the systems employed for this purpose is portrayed in figure 7.1.

Successful firms recognize that new product developments are likely to require development activities which are situation specific and which cannot be fully anticipated in laid down procedures. The first half of the development process is characterized by the team working out how to develop the concept and how the business definition might be improved. The second is characterized by tighter top management control – the team has worked out targets – and now has to perform to those targets.

Successful new product developers will often also experiment with their approaches. They can do this because activities such as partnering allow them to chop and change midstream without major cost consequences. The lesson to be drawn from the examples and practices of successful firms is that firms wishing to pursue new product development should adopt the loose-tight approach to the systems used in development. This allows a team to work up a business definition and to gather market information on the way it perceives to be most effective. Thereafter, once the business concept has been defined and accepted, the team is exposed to more rigorous checks.

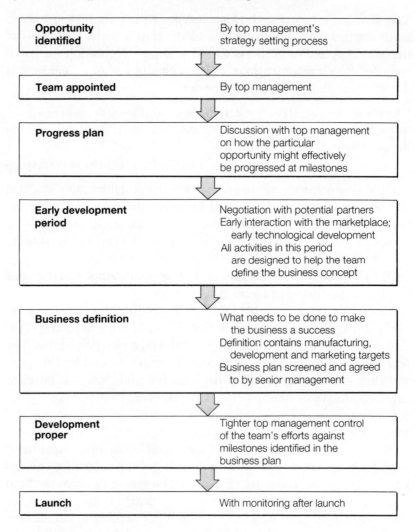

Figure 7.1:
The new product development system.

Conclusion

In this chapter and in the previous one we have built on the straight reporting of results by analysing more descriptively and prescriptively how to manage product improvement and new product development. We have demonstrated that the management of product change is highly dependent on the nature of the development task. High achieving firms explicitly address this issue and instigate different managerial methods and techniques for new product development, such as the following:

- **A loose-tight strategy:** Broad business opportunities and objectives are mapped out by projecting long-term trends in markets and technologies. New product opportunities are identified by an innovative assessment of core competences.
- **Top management leadership:** Top management leads new product development efforts through hands-on involvement in individual projects.
- **Supra-divisional structures:** Business teams are assembled to develop new products outside the mainstream organization. The purpose of such teams is to build a new business.
- **Intrapreneurs:** Development teams are staffed and led by intrapreneurs: managers who can envision new business opportunities and deal professionally and personally with the risks and uncertainties of new product development.
- **Free-wheeling systems:** Development teams are not encumbered by procedural strait-jackets: they are free to pursue new product developments in the way they think appropriate to meet overall strategic goals.

It will be noticed that the profile of management is quite different from that for the less risky and more certain task of product improvement. Tailoring managerial practices to different development tasks is of vital importance. For instance, the loose and flexible procedures characteristic of new product development would prove inefficient and ineffective for managing product improvement.

8

Managing Product Changes in Multi-business Firms

So far we have concentrated on activities involved with the development of improved and completely new products, with attention being focused almost exclusively on the operations of individual businesses. The purpose of this chapter is to draw together important recent trends on managing product changes in the context of multi-business operations. The chapter quite deliberately takes in the wider context of strategy and management in multi-business and multinational firms, with an emphasis on the three key tenets of successful product development: (1) markets, (2) top management leadership, and (3) effective teamwork.

Managing in a multi-business context is an important issue. Individual businesses in large corporations can rarely pursue their operations in isolation. While a business may be encouraged to act independently within a financial control firm, a time will usually come when assistance from head office is needed, particularly for funding expensive new product initiatives. Also, most managers are likely to find themselves in businesses or business units in which they are asked at certain points of time to take into consideration the interests of other businesses.

In chapter 4 we outlined different approaches or styles for managing constituent parts of large organizations. Three main approaches were discussed:

- Strategic planning or 'orchestrating'
- Strategic control or 'coaching'
- Financial control

The number of corporations which exclusively practise a financial control style in relation to their constituent businesses is likely to be small. It is anyway doubtful whether financial control firms do steadfastly stick to managing all businesses in a completely hands-off manner in the face of converging technologies and markets.

For example, Christopher Lorenz of the Financial Times has provided useful insights into the way Electrolux, the Swedish multinational, manages its operations through adopting distinctly different parenting roles for businesses in different stages of development. On being shown a diagram of ideal parenting roles for different types of businesses, with clear distinctions between (1) financial control, (2) strategic control, and (3) fully-fledged strategic planning, Anders Scharp, chief executive of Electrolux, is reported to have observed: 'Well, we really do all three!'[1]

In this chapter we look at issues currently facing managers at the multi-business level that have relevance to the management of product change. Increasingly, the driving force behind these issues is the existence of global competition. Such competition requires the closer working together by all constituent parts of multi-business concerns to capitalize on wider market opportunities.

The importance of global competition

In a sense, all Western businesses now compete on a global basis. They do so either directly by selling and manufacturing in an array of world markets, or indirectly because they find themselves at the receiving end, in their traditional markets, of actions undertaken by competitors who operate on a global basis. Across a wide range of industries, in both Britain and America, firms now feel the effects of such global competition. At present competition comes mainly from Japanese and Korean firms, but in time other Far Eastern competitors can be expected to enter this arena with increasing force.

Some relatively protected industries in Britain and America, such as food manufacturing, have yet to experience the full brunt of global competition. However, even in these industries there is increasing unease at the prospect of heightened foreign competition. Today all firms are potentially at risk from global competitors and therefore an understanding of global business warfare is important for those that want to survive and prosper in the longer term.

In terms of managing product change profitably, few firms can now turn their backs on global markets, because home markets are often too small in size to recoup the investment expenditures required for major developments. This has led more and more manufacturing firms to consider the potential offered by global markets. For such firms it becomes imperative to understand how multi-business operations can be linked together to maximize value chain synergies. In the context of the management of product change, there are three critical operational questions:

- What sort of global product development strategies work best?
- To what extent can headquarters, customers, and suppliers help with product developments?
- How can appropriate decisions be taken quickly?

In addressing these three critical issues, we have also drawn from insights generated by recent studies into multi-national and multi-business operations. Our own study concentrated on the management of product change within individual business units, which represents a complex and intricate phenomenon in itself. However, our motivation for exploring the present issues stems from comments made by some of the more enthusiastic respondents.

A large number of managers emphasized how the policies of the corporate centre can both inhibit and facilitate product change. Additionally, many respondents stressed that long-term competitive success does not lie with the pursuit of domestic markets alone. In more and more product markets, and particularly in high-technology markets, it is now essential to compete on a global basis.

We turn now to considering the three specific issues that are the concern of this chapter. Each is important in its own right, although it will become evident that all are closely interrelated. Not surprisingly, it is firms that address all questions in a co-ordinated and consistent way that stand the highest chance of managing long-run product development successfully.

Selecting a global product development strategy

The essence of business strategy is to build competitive advantage. At best, this will involve creating tomorrow's competitive advantages faster than competitors are able to copy. Earlier chapters have provided evidence which suggests that there are now firms that are much more skilled at this activity than others.

Successful competitive strategies flow from ambition or 'vision' provided by top management. We have shown in earlier chapters that such ambition, or vision needs to be underpinned by explicit planning to release the resources necessary to fulfil and drive the vision. This is especially important when ambitions exceed resources currently available.

It is important to emphasize that planning the allocation of resources is no substitute for objective setting. Objective setting and strategy determination are quite different from, and indeed are much greater activities, than planning. In our high achiever firms it was top management which provided the objectives that are the starting point for the whole competitive management process.

Top management must supply vision: planning is not enough

A great danger exists that top management's vision will not extend beyond satisfying the short-term objectives of shareholders and keeping raiders at bay. This risk is particularly strong in British and American corporations which are routinely required to account to shareholders on very short time horizons – certainly much shorter than is the case in most Japanese or West German firms. When top management is required to focus on short-term financial results, insufficient attention is often given to wider market developments. In these circumstances stagnation can easily become a self-fulfilling prophecy with markets becoming labelled as 'mature' because sales growth in them has plateaued through lack of interest and imagination from the top.

When this occurs, many firms rely on planning for the purpose of effecting a fit between existing opportunities and existing resources. But because of lack of vision on the part of top management, wider market opportunities may be misread, underestimated or not seen at all. What has happened in such cases is that top management's conception of an industry has matured – not the industry itself – and no amount of planning from headquarters or elsewhere will overcome this problem.

Canon's entry into the British and American copying market illustrates the power of a visionary approach, as opposed to a mechanistic planning-based approach. For many years it was Xerox which successfully sold a wide range of copiers in both countries using a direct salesforce of considerable size and cost. Canon reconceptualized the market by redesigning copiers so that these could be sold via office product retailers, which obviated the need for national sales forces. The new distribution strategy succeeded because great efforts had been made to make Canon copiers more reliable and simpler. By aiming high, but thinking deep, Canon's top management was able to side-step and nullify Xerox's distribution strengths by making them irrelevant to the market segments that were growing fastest.

When the intent of top management is extremely ambitious, there may be considerable gaps between what is aimed for and the resources available. It is in these circumstances that 'heroic management' is called for. Its task is to challenge the organization to close the gap, not by planning alone, but by commitment on the part of everyone to change. Exhortations are unlikely to be sufficient for this purpose. When the gap between available resources and what is needed is very great, skilful leaders now commonly set a series of attainable 'mini' goals for key groups of persons. For example, rather than aim to turn a corporation around in one go, some leaders set a limited agenda which focuses on specific manageable topics such as:

- Quality
- Product development
- Market development

Mini-goals have critical characteristics. They are not focused solely on markets, functions, or products. They are designed to improve the organization's capabilities in a 'generic' sense, by allowing it to pursue new and unconventional competitive strategies quickly and easily.

It is important for changes aimed at achieving mini goals or attainable 'chunks' to be negotiated with co-workers. For while achievement of specific ends may seem obvious to top management, a great deal of time is likely to be required in persuading the rest of the organization. This is where communication skills are of the utmost importance, and are given very great attention in successful firms – not only for formal planning purposes between headquarters and constituent businesses – but also for the informal lobbying which must accompany any change program.

The simple niche strategy trap

'Pursuit of a niche strategy is fine if the aim is to dominate a global niche rather than a simple domestic niche' was a statement made to us in one of our high achiever firms which operates on a global basis. In this firm it was explained that simple niches are vulnerable to competitors with a broader vision of market opportunities, and particularly to those who are prepared to exploit synergies between national markets. Our discussions in Japanese firms readily confirmed the basis for this fear, because really aggressive global players are now prepared to cross-subsidize national business operations for the purpose of building up a strong presence in particular product markets.

There are two important but interrelated issues involved: (1) interpretation of market trends for product development; that is to say, identifying emerging market opportunities to which new offerings can be directed; and (2) the degree of global competition.

When competition is conducted on a global basis, limited vision or aspirations on the part of top management can be extremely dangerous. At worst, it can lead firms to use tools of analysis, like portfolio planning, that are suited to assessing performance in rigidly circumscribed markets, but not in markets that enterprising vision can turn upside-down. The great disadvantage of portfolio planning is that it focuses attention on the supply side, and not on emerging possibilities. Concentrating attention solely on the supply side, particularly for the purpose of identifying strategic fit with existing operations, has led many businesses to seek salvation in pursuing a niche strategy in established markets.

While the pursuit of a simple (often domestic) niche strategy may be realistic for managers being appraised on short-term results, it can be dangerous for the longer-term interests of a business. To concentrate on just a very small part of the potential market for the purpose of generating profits is bound to be limiting. However, notwithstanding these limitations, many businesses continue to seek salvation in pursuing a simple niche strategy. This is in large part because the performance of most British and American corporations continues to be appraised primarily on the basis of short-term profitability.

Any business can increase its short-term profitability by cutting costs and engaging in so-called 'denominator management' to increase profits.[2] Unfortunately, while many British and American businesses have been forced to concentrate on this type of performance, the headquarters of many Japanese corporations have concentrated on studying how different national markets are evolving, and how opportunities within and across them can be reconceptualized to serve global ambitions.

As has been stressed in earlier chapters, successful product change often takes longer than short-term planning cycles which are still commonly used to steer many British and American businesses. It is in this area that headquarters influence can be especially valuable in providing a wider and also a longer-term horizon. There can be little doubt that traditional business unit structures inhibit the co-ordination of activities across individual businesses and markets and that this can make them vulnerable. Their vulnerability is neatly summed up in the statement made by a senior executive in a successful global company:

We're glad when we find a competitor managing by the portfolio concept – we can almost predict how much share we'll have to take away to put the business on the CEO's 'sell list'.[3]

Aim for new global niches with strong brands

In today's fast-changing markets successful long-term strategies are likely to be based increasingly on competitive initiation and not merely on competitive imitation. And, in many industries, long-term success will increasingly be linked to performance in a global market rather than in a simple domestic market.

Businesses which compete globally, or which are faced with competition from global players, will only understand their own vulnerability if they make determined efforts to study the competitive intentions of rivals. Unfortunately, many Western companies have misinterpreted the strategies of Japanese firms by watching closely only a few competitive tactics, such as cost of manufacture or quality. However, these are often the symptoms and not the causes of Japanese competitive success. They are often the result of implementing carefully selected competitive instruments stemming from market-led envisioning orchestrated by head offices.

As was stressed to us in several high achiever British and American businesses, strategies aimed at building competitive global advantages will at best be the result of having appraised target market opportunities afresh, rather than having been based solely on refinements to established market practices. Further, the choice of strategies is no longer as wide as it used to be. For example, concentrating on low-cost manufacturing is now an unattractive method of competing globally for most British and American firms, because it is easily copied by new entrants from low-cost producing countries. Concentrating on strong channels, on the other hand, presents a less vulnerable strategy, because channel strengths are more difficult to copy in the short term.

Potentially, the strongest strategy open to multi-business corporations today is building up strong global brands which can support a whole range of product lines offered by constituent businesses. The ideal model appears to be building up brands which are underpinned by core competences – as has been achieved by many successful Japanese firms like NEC, Fujitsu, Panasonic (Matsushita), Toshiba, Sony, Seiko, Sharp, Sanyo, Epson, Canon, Minolta and Honda.

In fact, global branding affords benefits at two levels. First, umbrella brands provide strong global market presence, reputation and market leverage. Second, under this umbrella a multi-business firm can then exploit advantages resulting from regional manufacturing and design centres, so that products can be tailored more closely to local markets. This policy is currently being successfully pursued by a number of Japanese firms. What such companies are doing is breaking certain commonly accepted 'rules' of strategy. For example, they pursue low-cost manufacturing and differentiation simultaneously, which is expressly advised against by some business strategy experts.[4] However, they do this successfully by strengthening their world presence in the eyes of customers through corporate branding; moving away from standardized world products where it is competitively advantageous to do so, and by providing markets with more carefully targeted new products than could otherwise be the case.

Essentially, what really successful global players do is to create a whole new space or market for themselves which is uniquely suited to their business strengths. This is much more than finding a niche within an established market. Frequently, the type of space created is off an established product market map; and, as was explained in chapter 2, for this reason is less vulnerable to imitation. This new

way of approaching opportunities is becoming increasingly important in markets where rapidly changing technology, deregulation
and globalization have undermined the value of traditional industry
analysis.

Global niching, then, presents considerable opportunities for
ambitious multi-business firms to redraw the competitive map in
their own favour. This will be possible only if they are capable and
ready to think outside traditional industry boundaries. The new
approach is quite different from simple domestic niching. While the
approach is sometimes referred to as exploiting a profitable niche,
the distinguishing feature of such new operations is the wider global
view of emerging opportunities.

Faced with this new type of competition, defensive minded manufacturers, with no real appreciation of alternative competitive strategies, are often doomed to a perpetual game of catch-up with more
skilful competitors. Unfortunately for them, strategies based on
imitation are readily apparent, especially to adversaries who have
already mastered these. Not surprisingly, by competing in completely new ways Japanese companies have recently been able to
creep up on traditional players in their home markets almost
unnoticed. This is because the new competitive approach mostly
avoids direct confrontation, concentrating instead on a completely
new set of competitive moves, which many traditional players have
often not even dreamed about.

The lesson to be drawn by managers in businesses that want
to succeed is to engage in 'competitive innovation', rather than
'competitive imitation'. The essence of competitive innovation is to
create tomorrow's competitive advantages faster than competitors
can mimic the advantages of today. The message is:

Don't just try to do better with what you have got (which represents an
asset-based simple planning approach), but try to configure completely
new ways of competing in chosen markets.

The markets chosen will need to be defined differently from the
way traditional players conceive them. Increasingly, they are
defined in terms of usage contexts (such as eating out occasions;
premium private travel; convenience eating; casual wear). And, to
reap economies in competing in a newly defined market, many
firms now automatically think in terms of entering several overseas
geographical markets, rather than simply exploiting a few.

Essentially, the new approach to competing globally relies on brains rather than brawn. It is admirably illustrated by the British electronics firm Amstrad which has an excellent record of conceptualizing market opportunities and supplying these with products which are often manufactured by third parties. It does this first through careful analysis of emerging market opportunities both at home and abroad, and second by developing appropriate offerings which are reinforced with strong umbrella brand names.

Reconciling inputs from headquarters, customers and suppliers

When it comes to managing product change, a business needs to recognize that the physical product is often only one part of a total delivery system. The actions and policies of suppliers and customers can all affect the innovative capacity of the offering 'system', as was explained in chapter 2. In this respect each element of the delivery chain needs to be carefully managed and integrated to generate the greatest possible innovative potential. Manufacturers with conservative and insular attitudes often pursue low-risk minor product changes. In a multi-business firm this managerial problem may be compounded by directives from the corporate centre. All of these elements give rise to potentially conflicting pressures for change. A strategic question which therefore needs to be addressed by all businesses is the extent to which suggestions from various sources – headquarters, customers and suppliers – should be acted upon.

The role of headquarters

For the purpose of competing globally, headquarters will often want to take responsibility in some decision areas, while leaving individual business units in charge of others. As has already been stressed, global competition in manufactured products can benefit from a broad concept of a product line which the headquarters' viewpoint is ideally able to provide. Headquarters can encourage world-scale manufacturing, world-scale distribution and global brands. However, world-scale distribution and branding are likely to be economical only if the company has a wide and growing range of products. Hence, it is likely to be firms that develop a continuous stream of new products that can best justify the high cost of world brands and their distribution.

In several of our high achiever firms, we saw how responsibility for global competitive strategy is separated from responsibility for business competitive strategy. Individual businesses are charged with developing some aspects of the marketing mix, while headquarters take the lead in co-ordinating the strategic visions of local operations. In this way headquarters can advise on the timing of new product launches, and on the targeted level of market shares in particular markets, taking into account likely competitive actions and reactions from world competitors.

Potentially this presents conflicts between:

- Individual business units and country managers
- Country managers and product co-ordinators
- Country managers and international marketing co-ordinators

The key to changing harmful conflicts into constructive action is communication and participation. Headquarters have a key role to play in this. At best, headquarters will communicate the strategic vision of the whole firm, so that individual business units can recognize, understand and complement the core driving strategy. In order to do this successfully, individual businesses will need to be involved in strategy formulation. When this is done really well, headquarters activities can both drive and support individual business plans, and so help in capitalizing on supply-side synergies.

Taking a lead from customers

We have seen in previous chapters how high achiever firms follow a predominantly market-led approach to product development. It is important to emphasize that the success results much more from proactive market interpretation rather than from lamely following the suggestions of key customers.

This issue is important, because several analysts have shown that customers can play an important part in identifying opportunities for profitable product change.[5] Meeting customers' needs is, of course, a prerequisite for successful product change. Nevertheless, a danger exists that a business may end up acting as nothing more than a sub-contractor for key customers, and in this way lose control over its own destiny. It is here that headquarters has an especially important role to play in guarding against businesses being led astray by customers. The danger occurs principally in industrial markets where individual customers can be very powerful indeed. However, the problem also arises in another guise in consumer markets where big retailing chains exert major market power.

For a business to utilize, rather than be totally driven by customers, requires an assessment of two different market dynamics. On the one hand, the business needs to discriminate between different types of customers. Customers who are innovators and market leaders in their own marketplaces are likely to be a critical source of new product ideas. Other types of customer are likely to be less strategically useful, suggesting only incremental and low-risk product changes, which support their own limited marketplace thrust. Importantly, emerging trends in the marketplace as a whole need to be weighed against individual customer suggestions. To be competitively successful new products must attract sufficient market support. The trick is, therefore, to utilize innovative customers in the context of the demands and constraints of emerging markets.

Involving suppliers

Not only do customers have the potential to inhibit or to facilitate product change, but the contribution of suppliers can also be critical in this process.

Many successful corporations have now decided to supply an increasingly wide array of products so that these can be tailored as closely as possible to the demands of target markets. Japanese car manufacturers are leading the way in this by offering a very wide variety of models from one assembly line. They do this by approaching the manufacturing process in completely new ways with the help of selected suppliers with whom they work very closely indeed.

Several commentators have shown that certain Western businesses are now adopting and refining Japanese manufacturing techniques to provide the flexibility to improve products quickly and cheaply. One method relies on involving suppliers to develop parts needed to complete product improvements. In this way component suppliers, whose labour costs are lower than those of the car-makers, are now being involved in designing and assembling modules which are incorporated wholesale into the finished product.[6]

To encourage suppliers to help in product development in this way, some car manufacturers now offer exclusive supply contracts. Consequently, suppliers become locked into a long-term relationship to ensure standards are consistent with the strategic aspirations of manufacturers. All this is very different from the multiple sourcing arrangements of the past, when car-makers used their purchasing power to squeeze every last penny out of the unit prices quoted by component suppliers. The great advantage of involving suppliers in modular product developments is that 'manufacturers' can concentrate on their real areas of expertise – marketing, distribution and design. In other words, they can concentrate on putting together offerings which are appropriate to the markets being targeted.

By managing and co-operating with supply systems in this way, the activities of suppliers become powerful additions to the capabilities of the entire delivery system. To be really effective, such action may need to be driven by the corporate centre. Not only does this generate leverage across the whole market system, but it can also lend credibility to proposals for other activities, such as joint research and development. In this way the entire delivery system can become more responsive to potentially profitable changes in selected markets. With a comprehensive and well thought-through supply chain, innovative companies can thereby both steal a march on, and protect their lead over, less skilled competitors.

Empowering businesses to take quick decisions

Currently most strategic management theory and almost all corporate planning systems are based on the assumption that it is corporate goals which guide the strategies of individual business units, and that such business strategies will guide functional tactics. Under this model, top management of both the corporation as a whole and of individual businesses is seen as making strategy. Middle-level managers then execute strategies. However, with the increasing ambiguity and complexity which surrounds global marketing decisions, it is likely that top management will no longer be able to do all the envisioning alone.

We were made aware in several leading firms that the strategy-hierarchy model can undermine business unit competitiveness. This is because it fosters an over-elitist view of management which disenfranchises the very persons who might contribute to product and business growth. As a result of being excluded from key decision making, executives may fail to identify with corporate goals or, worse still, with business unit goals.

This is one of the main reasons why the old style leadership cult is beginning to be questioned. In many of our high achiever firms it is becoming recognized that, while top management is always likely to be looked upon to set the ultimate goals of a corporation, and of individual business ventures within it, greater humility on the part of leaders may be a first step in revitalizing old style corporations. There is, after all, likely to be lots of knowledge in an organization just waiting to be tapped. Certainly in many firms we visited we came across many middle-level managers who had long ago envisaged more progressive ways forward – certainly long before more enlightened top management was formally appointed to change things.

New styles of leadership

A key question which arises is how much of a loner the top manager can afford to be. Here the work of Waterman (co-author of *In Search of Excellence*) is of relevance. In researching the features of successful 'renewing' organizations, he found that while all such firms have a chief executive who is clearly in charge, seldom is he or she a grand-standing figure. Importantly, it was found that it is the team at the top which makes for successful corporate renewal:[7]

A company that has good teamwork and co-operation at the top enjoys a terrific multiplier effect: that close-knit gang of three or four accomplishes far more than does a throng of managers (and supporting retinues and overheads) three times its size. Teamwork companies enjoy a communication level that seems uncanny to outsiders; important ideas move like quicksilver. Decisions are made in hallways and on telephones. Formal meetings are less frequent and are not all that formal.

Burns, in his classic book *Leadership*, provides a framework for understanding recent trends. He argues that 'transactional' leaders give followers a sense of purpose for which they are prepared to yield certain power. But that it is 'transforming leadership' which raises the sights and aspirations of followers to a higher level. While both types of leader can contribute to human purpose, transforming leaders elevate the aspirations of followers in such a way that allows both them and the organization to grow.[8]

We saw evidence in all high achiever firms of determined efforts on the part of top management to involve a wider spread of co-workers. Nevertheless, irrespective of how much power top management is prepared to share, top management alone remains responsible for the following tasks:

- Establish: (1) corporate vision, (2) clear milestones and regular review mechanisms.
- Move forward in steps or 'chunks' that are intelligible to other personnel.
- Develop a competitor focus at every level.
- Create a sense of excitement, purpose and urgency.
- Ensure employees are provided with the necessary skills through training.

New organizational structures

As companies have globalized their operations, strenuous efforts have been made to combine the efficiency resulting from functional specialization with the responsiveness of businesses focused on selected markets. The early solution was the management matrix in which executives had two bosses: one in charge of satisfying a particular market, another in charge of a particular function. In practice many corporations found the matrix resulted in much confusion and endless rounds of meetings.[9]

As we saw earlier, companies that have embraced the concept of focusing their organization squarely on perceived business opportunities have swept aside whole tiers of management. The resulting flatter organization does require top management to understand the work of far more subordinates. Interestingly, in several high performing firms we were given the distinct impression that the modern manager regards himself less as someone of importance in the official hierarchy, than as someone working successfully with others over whom he has no direct authority.

We saw evidence in successful firms that traditional functional structures are being replaced by new evolving ones, which are multi-dimensional. However, just as was seen with the advent of matrix structures in the late 1970s, these new complex structures will only work if people want them to work – hence the importance of shared values.

What struck us most about successful firms was that people now appear to matter much more than structures. That is not to say that there is no conflict in new style organizations. However, the conflicts which arise are of a constructive nature. Indeed, it is of considerable interest that Klaus Brockhoff, a professor at Kiel University, has found that the most successful product innovator firms in a sample of West German manufacturers were those in which constructive conflict between marketing and technical personnel was tolerated. This is an important finding which flies in the face of naive notions of harmony between functions in successful product development.[10]

For the purpose of encouraging best results we observed that, in certain firms, 'shoot-outs' are now deliberately set up to see which solution will work best in the real world. However, in these firms, the emphasis is on open competition – free from the 'win at someone else's expense' mentality. On the other hand, in traditional organizations there is often a tendency to attempt to solve complex problems through structures which suppress conflict. Effective organizations confront conflicts constructively: in them managers are learning to live with the greater degrees of ambiguity which now typify more and more complex tasks such as product development.

Networking

In high achiever firms we found evidence that bureaucratic structures are being replaced by networking. By this we mean that previously established tightly circumscribed procedures are being replaced by looser 'facilitating processes'. Firms that are doing this are becoming leaner, fitter and faster. The way results are achieved is by the top person (or top team) 'empowering' co-workers to take independent day-to-day decisions. This can only be effective if the people at the top have taken the trouble to spell-out the overall direction in the first place. Leaders in such firms do not tell co-workers exactly what to do. Much rather, they encourage co-workers to think out solutions for themselves.

We believe that encouraging co-workers to think for themselves and empowering them to act will become increasingly necessary in product development as the environment changes at a faster pace.

Indeed, it is just because of these fast and complicated changes that top managers will need more and more help in interpreting opportunities. Hence, the leader of the 1990s is likely to be someone who will take the broad view, and know when to give away his authority, rather than only give orders. Above all, he or she will need to be a skilled negotiator and will need to manage without resorting to old style controls.

In a sense networking – one of the latest trends in organization – implies almost a non-organization. The theory behind networking is that a business is little more than a network of persons with specialized skills. As opportunities are spotted, the business shapes itself into whatever form is necessary to exploit these.

Rather than accepting networking as a new dogma which will suit all parts of a business, we observed that enlightened firms are using networks in different shapes and forms as best suits the tasks being addressed. The most flamboyant example of a network is the *self-managing team*, the purpose of which is to accomplish a major task that is different from what most persons in an ongoing business are working on. IBM's first personal computer was the outcome of such a network. Working outside the normal corporate bureaucracy it not only developed one of IBM's most successful new products, but also did so in record time.

Other examples of networks are *problem-solving teams* of volunteers who meet for a few hours every week in order to address particular tasks. Based on the Japanese quality circle concept, these teams have no power to implement findings, but are the source of major competitive initiatives, such as product improvements.

Special-purpose teams, on the other hand, represent a half-way stage between self-managing and problem-solving teams. Their task is commonly to introduce new technology; new working practices, or new product lines. While these and other forms of teams were used by only a few firms in the 1970s and 1980s, the current trend is most definitely towards exploiting the advantages offered by this form of networking.

Creating the responsive organization

In conditions of faster and increasingly complex changes, businesses will need to learn on a continuing basis if they are to survive. Successful survival will require decision making to be closer to the customer. Because hierarchical organizations are slower to respond to market changes, it is likely that businesses will need to rely increasingly on decentralized decision making. The real test of an effective organization will therefore be whether it holds up under the pressures imposed by complex and constant changes.

Flexible organizations are able to concentrate on core market-related activities. In them, access to needed skills will ideally be seen as more beneficial than ownership of such skills. After all, important peripheral activities can always be hived-off to outside specialists, as was seen in the examples of novel new product development practices described in chapters 4 and 7.

In a competitive world where markets and technologies can be restructured very quickly, it is the people in a firm who matter most, *not* the existing organization structure. Hence the truly responsive organization is one which identifies how each individual can best contribute in battles for target markets through effective teamwork.

However, in addition to willing and well-motivated staff who are ready to respond quickly to emerging market trends, there is a need for realistic schemes of analysis. In this respect, it is critically important how a multi-business firm defines the markets in which it wants to compete. It is, after all, in markets that operating profits are made or lost. Some analysts, such as the McKinsey consultant Kenichi Ohmae have advanced the concept of 'strategic planning units' for defining competitive arenas. The purpose of such strategic planning units is to focus efforts on markets which can be attacked quickly with products from different constituent units.[11]

Basically, the concept of strategic planning units is similar to that of categories of markets which is in common usage in fast-moving consumer goods manufacturing firms. Examples of categories of demand are snack foods; convenience eating; premium private auto-mobile travel, etc. The situation becomes complicated when categories of demand are supplied with corporate products from different operating units. There is, after all, no reason why a corporate product cannot be offered to more than one category of demand. For example, a certain cereal might be used both as a breakfast food and also as a snack, both of which represent distinct categories of demand.

We found several high achiever multi-business firms now actively experimenting with better ways for identifying profitable categories of demand. This task is critical, as has already been stressed, because it will define the way in which the corporation as a whole sets itself up to compete. Careful determination of strategic planning units will allow multi-business firms to overcome the disadvantages of simple product improvement which at worst results in excessive emphasis on supply-side factors, meaning that emerging markets are not exploited as fast as they might be.

Conclusion

Adopting a strategic planning unit approach to product development has important potential implications for the future shape of multi-business firms that want to compete globally. We anticipate that in the next decade it is likely that several large and proud corporations will turn themselves into brokerages of sorts. Their business headquarters are likely to become small and will specialize on design and distribution for those markets in which they want to compete. Sales and manufacturing activities are likely to be sub-contracted.

If these developments do, in fact, materialize, it will become the critical activity in such firms to read emerging market opportunities accurately. Whether this is best done from a head office or some other vantage point in the organization will depend on a multitude of operational and competitive factors. One thing is certain, however, once fully implemented, the concept of strategic planning units presents not only exciting, but also disruptive opportunities. The analytical emphasis will fall where it should be: on identifying and exploiting market opportunities, rather than on supply-side factors. It is likely, therefore, to lead to spinning-off of many supply-side operations, as firms concentrate on what they understand best. It may be just the sort of thinking which will regain for some of today's over-large corporations the focus which allowed them to grow into profitable businesses in the past.

It will be obvious that in this chapter we have stepped out from the confines of our fieldwork. We have done so to look at the broader issues of multi-business management and how the complexity introduced by competing globally might be managed best. Such issues are assuming increasing importance in a complex and changing modern environment and directly impact on the innovative capability and direction of individual business units. In the final chapter we shall reiterate our key findings in this area, as well as highlighting issues that require further research so that understanding of the complex and intricate phenomenon of product change can be improved.

9

Conclusions: Critical Findings and Outstanding Questions

THE purpose of this chapter is to draw together the themes in previous chapters to provide an overview of the management of product change in large established corporations. Key findings are summarized and critical issues are highlighted which require further research.

Critical findings

Like all research based on direct interviews, the findings detailed in this book have limitations. Our findings are only as good as the information provided by the managers we spoke with. The study was deliberately confined to British and American companies, manufactured product markets, and focused on the actions and policies of individual business units.

We believe, however, that our broad-based study has generated insights into the rich complexity of product development management which are relevant to many different fields of manufacturing. We will now distil these insights into a short list of key factors.

Product change should be market-based

It is clear that many firms are placing increased emphasis on product change as a means for rejuvenating and securing long-term competitive growth. In the face of rapidly changing competitive environments and fast-changing technologies, skilful organic product development represents a robust competitive strategy.

To drive product change effectively, firms need to pursue a new approach. Strategies for product development need to be market-based, not just asset-based. In this way firms can successfully capitalize on emerging market trends and redraw industry boundaries and competitive conditions in their favour. A market-based approach requires top management to step outside the confines and thinking of the current business and to point the way forward by inspiring and motivating those around them.

Market-based product change in multi-business firms that compete globally can benefit considerably from strategic direction and co-ordination from the corporate centre. It is for this reason that we would advocate the strategic planning or, at least, the strategic control style in such firms. Product development is too important an activity to be left to the unco-ordinated independent efforts of different parts of large corporations. However, as has already been amply emphasized, success will not result from making a few critical changes to the way the product development program is handled. In pursuit of product change, firms need to understand and handle six critical dimensions simultaneously.

Focus proactively on competitive market opportunities

Successful product change depends on an understanding of evolving markets and the dynamics operating within those markets. To be effective, product change has to become an integral part of corporate strategy. It cannot be carried out in a strategic vacuum in which the initiative for new or improved products gravitates to customers or competitors.

Corporate strategy must identify the growth role of internal product change and what market opportunities can be best served by this means. Such a process encourages long-term thinking based on market analysis, which is much superior to a traditional rolling project-to-project approach.

Ideally, innovative market interpretation will be followed up with proactive competitive moves which leave the competition guessing at what is coming next from your product development stable.

Issues relating to the identification and effective exploitation of competitive product development options were examined in chapters 2, 3 and 5.

Link market opportunities to corporate asset strengths

The most successful product developments link the opportunities of the marketplace to core competences. This reduces risks while increasing the likelihood of strong, defensible product advantages. The critical difference between firms that are successful and less successful in doing this is the way corporate competences are conceptualized.

Firms that are less successful product developers understand their strengths only in terms of current markets, current operations and current products. High achievers, on the other hand, understand their strengths in a 'generic' sense: distribution, marketing skills, core technical competences and so on – in fact all the factors which differentiate their offering from that of competitors.

Generic strengths can be applied to a wide range of current and new market opportunities and success will result from innovative combinations of offerings. Far from constraining firms in their product development efforts, enlightened use of internal competences can lead to the identification of far more product development opportunities than was previously thought possible.

Issues relating to managing market opportunities in relation to core competences and strengths were examined in chapters 3 and 4.

Skilful management of the value chain

Core competences are not simply or solely derived from the company's own operation. The innovative capacity of a company is affected, and to a large extent determined by, the characteristics and capabilities of the value-added system within which it operates. This will encompass suppliers, its own operations, sub-contractors, distributors and customers.

Management needs to make decisions about supply-chain variables to ensure that suppliers become equally responsive to opportunities for product change. Similarly, lead customers need to be chosen with care to nurture partnerships which will enhance the innovative capability of the total system. In this way factors can be identified and managed which facilitate product change across the entire delivery system. Further, the actions and policies of suppliers and customers can be focused to enhance – and not to constrain – the development of new product opportunities.

Issues relating to synergies between value chains were examined in chapters 2, 7 and 8.

Collect marketing information on a global basis

In the future, long-term survival for many businesses is likely to depend on an ability to operate on a global basis. Expensive product changes often become cost effective only if directed to international demand. In these cases, market assessment on a global basis becomes the critical input into an effective strategy for product change. Businesses must become skilled at utilizing the information generated by diverse and geographically spread operating units. Further, head offices need to be capable of envisioning and encouraging global market opportunities on the basis of this type of information.

Issues relating to global competitiveness were examined in chapter 8.

Communicating vision internally

Product change disrupts current business operations and creates uncertainties in the minds of managers at all levels of an organization. Top management needs to communicate and explain the vision of where the business is going. It needs to ensure that product development options are perceived by the organization as being opportunities and not threats. Only in this way will commitment to and ownership of product change be recognized by those managers instrumental in its implementation.

Issues relating to top management's role in effecting product changes were examined in chapters 4, 6 and 7.

Encourage and reward teamwork

Product change is a complex process requiring the management and manipulation of many skill bases within and outside the firm. These skill bases need to be married to allow for the maximization of internal strengths and the minimization of delays and threats to product change caused by internal strife.

Product development is, of its nature, a problem-solving and iterative process in which a whole series of options and solutions need to be considered. Only through effective teamwork can product development be undertaken with anything like the speed necessary in most competitive environments.

Not only should teamwork be encouraged, it must also be rewarded. Some firms do this by allowing self-managing teams to grow into self-standing businesses. Such an approach ensures commitment and enthusiasm for product change and underpins thorough and systematic development work. The fundamental value of this approach is that it links personal and corporate development.

Issues relating to teamwork were examined in chapters 5 and 8.

Company approach not country of origin is important

We have found that product development success factors are company, not country-based. This is an important message, given the lip-service paid to the view that American companies are better than their British counterparts at managing. Certainly, American firms do appear to have a preference for more formal and thorough planning procedures, as well as for more explicit corporate strategies and mission statements. However, as we have seen, this is just one element of a complex managerial formula which needs to be applied to achieve effective product changes.

The evidence collected suggests that some companies, irrespective of national origin, are markedly more skilled at managing product changes than are others. Moreover, given the growth of global product development competition, national origins are likely to assume far less importance in the future.

Managerial efforts must be tailored to the task

While the factors listed above are applicable and useful to all types of product change, high achiever firms recognize that these factors can only generate a climate in which product change can be pursued purposefully. Such firms understand that detailed management practice needs to be tailored to the particular task; that is to say, type of product development being pursued. It is in this connection that the McKinsey 7Ss framework provides much guidance in both diagnosing and in prescribing the way forward.[1]

While top management has a critical role to play in all types of product development, in the case of *product improvements* it can best adopt a sponsoring, not authoritarian, meddlesome or *laissez-faire* style of control. Effective teams brought together for this purpose will have close links with the firm's existing operations and so ensure that major competences are capitalized on, and that implementation is smooth and efficient. Product improvement should thus be seen to be an integral part of current business operations and be managed as such.

For the inherently more risky and disruptive task of *new product development*, the 7Ss need to be managed differently. Here top management needs to adopt a leading, hands-on role. Ideally, supra-divisional agents of change are assembled in order to capitalize on the fresh business vision of intrapreneurs and other corporate visionaries. To allow this to happen, procedures need to be loosened up to handle new circumstances and uncertainties.

The managerial scenarios provided, particularly those in chapters 6 and 7, demonstrated clearly that there is no one magic formula for success in product change. However, we were able to highlight the principles of best practice in high achiever firms within the context of different markets, organizations and cultures. In particular, the approach of top management, and the establishment of effective teamworking, represent the core managerial dynamics of implementing successful product change.

Outstanding questions

While our investigation has contributed to increasing managerial understanding of how product change can best be managed, several critical issues remain which require further research. The most important of these are discussed below.

How can multi-business firms best manage global product change?

Chapter 8 demonstrated some of the critical managerial issues faced by the corporate centre. Given increasing global competition, it is necessary for corporations to both capitalize on global strengths and opportunities, while at the same time allowing constituent businesses (which are necessarily closest to their markets) to manage themselves efficiently. Such issues remain only partially understood by analysts, yet it is clear that they have a fundamental bearing on the long-term success of multi-business corporations.

Future research in this area must, in our opinion, lie in trying to understand better the approach and policies of world leaders in product change, particularly of leading Japanese and West German companies in selected industries. Such research is far more likely to reveal actionable findings of direct use to managers who now have to compete globally than are studies of solely national firms.

How can market opportunities best be identified?

Market-based product change requires unconventional ways of conceptualizing markets and emerging opportunities. As we have shown, standard techniques of market research are likely to work best in current and well-defined product markets. It is clear from our research that many companies rely on special insights, rather than on well-established techniques, to identify and anticipate markets that have not, as yet, been fully established.

A key question is whether the new techniques of analysis outlined in chapter 2 can be developed further to help market visionaries anticipate and quantify new opportunities more precisely. If this is not yet possible, then entrepreneurial firms will have to continue to rely on the chance skills of particularly gifted individuals in identifying new product development opportunities.

What is the best basis for funding technical development work?

Although we did not specifically address the issue of the percentage of sales turnover devoted to R&D in different businesses, we gained the impression that American firms on average spend twice as much on R&D than do British firms in the same types of businesses. While this impression is of some interest, we would maintain that it is not the absolute amounts of money spent on R&D activities which are important, but the way in which such expenditures are applied. We found widespread anecdotal evidence that in many successful businesses product change is not as dependent on R&D resources as is commonly thought. This is so, because getting a development to function efficiently in a technical sense may be a necessary precondition for market success, but it is certainly not the only or necessarily the most important factor contributing to commercial success.

Nevertheless, particularly in high technology product markets, considerable funds will continue to be needed to complete technical development work, and the precise basis on which such sums are allocated, released and managed throughout the development process requires further analysis. Given the complex strategic roles product change can fulfil, relevant techniques for measuring the appropriateness of various types of funding (particularly that released to corporate research laboratories) need to be developed.

Is product development different from new service development?

Our research confined itself to manufacturing companies, yet the service economy continues to develop at a faster pace in many developed countries. The theoretical concepts of service marketing are still to be firmly established in a way that can directly contribute to managerial practice and to competitive success. Knowledge is even more sparse in the case of new service development. Critical questions remain to be answered in this area, especially how service firms, with very close links with their customers, and whose 'product offering' is so variously perceived by customer groups, can best exert independent direction within product change programs.

Notes

1 Background to the Study

1 Pratten, C. (1986) The importance of giant companies. *Lloyds Bank Review*, January, 33–48.
2 Aldington, L. (1985) *Report from the Select Committee on Overseas Trade.* London: HMSO.
3 Grinyer, P. H. and Spender, J. C. (1979) Recipes, crises and adaptation in mature businesses. *International Studies of Management and Organization*, 9 (3), 113–33.
    Johnson, G. (1987) *Strategic Change and the Management Process.* Oxford: Basil Blackwell.

2 Product Development: the Strategic Choices

1 Levitt, T. (1980) Marketing success through differentiation – of anything. *Harvard Business Review*, 58 (1), 83–91.
2 de Bruicker, F. S. and Summe, G. L. (1985) Make sure your customers keep coming back. *Harvard Business Review*, 63 (1), 92–8.
3 Mathur, S. S. (1988) How firms compete: a new classification of generic strategies. *Journal of General Management*, 14 (1), 30–57.
4 Porter, M. (1985) *Competitive Advantage: Creating and Sustaining Superior Performance.* London: Collier Macmillan.
5 O'Hare, M. (1988) *Innovate! How to Gain and Sustain Competitive Advantage.* Oxford: Basil Blackwell.

3 How High Achievers Manage Product Change

1 Peters, T. J. and Waterman, R. H. (1982) *In Search of Excellence: Lessons from America's Best-run Companies.* New York: Harper & Row.

2 Pascale, R. T. and Athos, A. G. (1982) *The Art of Japanese Management.* London: Penguin Books.

3 Peters, T. J. and Waterman, R. H. (1982) *In Search of Excellence: Lessons from America's Best-run Companies.* New York: Harper & Row.

4 Johne, F. A. and Snelson, Patricia A. (1988) Success factors in product innovation: a selective review of the literature. *Journal of Product Innovation Management,* 5 (2), 114–28.

5 Takeuchi, H. and Nonaka, I. (1986) The new new product development game. *Harvard Business Review,* 64 (1), 137–46.

6 Porter, M. (1985) *Competitive Advantage: Creating and Sustaining Superior Advantage.* London: Collier Macmillan.

4 Top Management's Contribution

1 Cooper, R. G. and Kleinschmidt, E. J. (1987) New products, what separates winners from losers? *Journal of Product Innovation Management,* 4 (3), 169–84.

Johne, F. A. and Snelson, Patricia A. (1988) Success factors in product innovation: a selective review of the literature. *Journal of Product Innovation Management,* 5 (2), 114–28.

Hopkins, D. S. (1981) New product winners and losers. *Research Management* (May), 12–17.

Maidique, M. A. and Zirger, B. J. (1984) A study of success and failure in product innovation: the case of the US electronics industry. *IEEE Transactions in Engineering Management,* EM-31, (4), 192–203.

Quinn, J. B. (1986) Managing innovation: controlled chaos. *The McKinsey Quarterly* (Spring), 2–21.

Rothwell, R. (1979) Successful and unsuccessful innovators. *Planned Innovation* (April), 126–28.

Souder, W. E. (1981) Encouraging entrepreneurship in large corporations. *Research Management,* 24 (3), 18–22.

2 Booz, Allen & Hamilton (1982) *New Products Management for the 1980s.* New York: Booz, Allen & Hamilton.

3 Takeuchi, H. and Nonaka, I. (1986) The new new product development game. *Harvard Business Review,* 64 (1), 137–46.

4 Tushman, M. L. and Nadler, D. A. (1986) Organizing for innovation. *California Management Review,* XXVIII (3), 74–92.

5 Goold, M. and Campbell, A. (1987) *Strategies and Styles: The Role of the Centre in Managing Diversified Corporations.* Oxford: Basil Blackwell.

6 Harvey-Jones, J. (1988) *Making it Happen: Reflections on Leadership.* London: Collins.

7 Ohmae, K. (1982) *The Mind of the Strategist.* London: Penguin.

8 Drucker, P. F. (1979) *Management: Tasks, Responsibilities, Practices.* London: Pan.
9 Burgelman, R. A. (1984) Designs for corporate entrepreneurship in established firms. In G. Carroll and D. Vogel (eds), *Strategy and Organization: A West Coast Perspective.* Pitman: Boston.
10 Ohmae, K. (1982) *The Mind of the Strategist.* London: Penguin.

5 Using Teamwork to Complete Developments

1 Takeuchi, H. and Nonaka, I. (1986) The new new product development game. *Harvard Business Review,* 64 (1), 137–46.
2 Pugh, D. S. (1984) The measurement of organization structures: does context determine form? In *Organization Theory,* 2nd edn. Harmondsworth, Middlesex: Penguin, 67–86.
3 Booz, Allen & Hamilton (1982) *New Products Management for the 1980s.* New York: Booz, Allen & Hamilton.
  Cooper, R. G. (1983) A process model for industrial new product development. *IEEE Transactions in Engineering Management.* EM-30 (1), 2–11.
4 Pugh, D. S. (1984) The measurement of organization structures: does context determine form? In *Organization Theory,* 2nd edn. Harmondsworth, Middlesex: Penguin, 67–86.

7 Effective New Product Development Practice

1 Foster, R. N. (1986) *Innovation: The Attacker's Advantage.* London: Macmillan.
2 Peters, T. J. and Waterman, R. H. (1982) *In Search of Excellence: Lessons from America's Best-run Companies.* New York: Harper & Row.
3 Tushman, M. L. and Nadler, D. A. (1986) Organizing for innovation. *California Management Review,* XXVIII (3), 74–92.

8 Managing Product Changes in Multi-business Firms

1 Lorenz, C. (1989) Striving to exploit an elusive balance. *Financial Times,* June 19, p. 12.
2 Doyle, P. (1987) Marketing and the British chief executive. *Journal of Marketing Management,* 3 (2), 121–32.
3 Hamel, G. and Prahalad, C. K. (1989) Strategic intent. *Harvard Business Review,* 76 (2), 63–76.
4 Porter, M. (1985) *Competitive Advantage: Creating and Sustaining Superior Performance.* London: Collier Macmillan.

5 Hippel, E. von (1986) Lead users: a source of novel product concepts. *Management Science*, 32 (7), 32–47.

Shaw, B. (1985) The role of the interaction between the user and the manufacturer in medical equipment innovation. *R&D Management*, 15 (4), 283–92.

6 Hayes, R. H. (1988) *Dynamic Manufacturing: Creating the Learning Organization*. New York: Free Press.

Hayes, R. H. and Wheelwright, S. C. (1984) *Restoring Our Competitive Edge: Competing through Manufacturing*. New York: Wiley.

7 Waterman, R. H. (1987) *The Renewal Factor: How the Best get and keep Competitive Edge*. New York: Bantam Books.

8 Burns, J. M. (1979) *Leadership*. New York: Harper & Row.

9 Dumaine, B. (1989) What the leaders of tomorrow see. *Fortune*, July 3, 24–34.

10 Brockhoff, K. (1989) *Schnittstellen-Management*. Stuttgart: Poeschel Verlag.

11 Ohmae, K. (1982) *The Mind of the Strategist*. London: Penguin.

9 Conclusions: Critical Findings and Outstanding Questions

1 Peters, T. J. and Waterman, R. H. (1982) *In Search of Excellence: Lessons from America's Best-run Companies*. New York: Harper & Row.

Appendix 1

Method of Approaching Firms and Interview Schedule

Method of approaching firms

With hindsight it still amazes us that so many firms were prepared to talk about such a sensitive subject. To a large extent this reflects the trouble spent approaching target firms in the first place. Our experience leads us to conclude that technique in approaching firms for co-operation is of the utmost importance. For this reason we shall spend a little time on this topic in the hope that what we have learned will benefit others.

Initial attempts to gain entry to firms by means solely of telephone contact were singularly unsuccessful. The subject of our research was too complicated to be explained in the few moments one has available to introduce oneself when 'cold-calling' on the telephone. Managers are rightly suspicious of outsiders inquiring into anything to do with product development matters. Not surprisingly, requests made on the telephone to meet with not just a marketing manager, but also a technical manager, for the purpose of discussing product development procedures stand very little chance of success.

Our amended approach was far more successful. A personal letter was sent to the chief executive or president of the holding company explaining the purpose of the study and asking to be directed to the head of the operating unit concerned with developing new products for the markets in which we were interested. In instances when we were quite clear which division or business unit was involved, we wrote direct to its head.

In each case, including also the American firms in our sample, we volunteered to call the chief executive's office (or the head of the operating unit) a few days after sending our letter to ascertain whether the firm was prepared to co-operate with us. On telephoning head office we were usually told that our letter had been passed to the chief of the appropriate operating unit. Thereafter, a common approach was pursued. In each case the chief of the operating unit was telephoned so that any questions about our proposal might be answered there and then, and an appointment was made to visit.

In instances when firms decided not to co-operate, a letter would usually wing its way back to us quite fast, and we regarded that as the end of the matter. Various reasons were given. Procter & Gamble in Cincinnati, Ohio were not untypical in refusing, saying: 'we regard our product development process, particularly the principles which guide that process, as proprietary'.

Sometimes our letter, which requested a meeting with a policy maker and an operating manager was passed to the respective policy maker, whom we then contacted on the telephone. It then became a job of skilfully selling the benefits of the study prior to making an appointment for a series of personal visits.

One important reason why we believe we were so successful in gaining co-operation from target firms was because our study was offered on a syndicated basis. All co-operating firms were promised a copy of the findings – a promise which we fulfilled as the first part of our objective to communicate findings to those who would find greatest benefit from them: managers concerned with product development.

Whenever we were denied co-operation, a substitute firm was approached from a list of reserves which had been prepared during the desk research part of the study. We were fortunate in gaining co-operation from most of the British target firms. The situation with American firms was different. There we were met with far more suspicion for two apparent reasons. First, there was suspicion that we might be spying on their operations (which in a sense we were). Second, few American firms felt that they had much to learn from British practices.

In some cases we were told that co-operation might well have been given for a syndicated study of firms in the same industry, but not for a cross-industry study. We thought at the time, and feel this even more strongly now, that this reflects a singularly inward-looking attitude which fewer and fewer firms can nowadays afford.

INTERVIEW SCHEDULE

INDUSTRY SECTOR:		
PRODUCT MARKET:		
COMPANY NAME	PARENT	DIVISION/SBU
	SBU for SECTION B responses:	
Main Products:		

CONTROL VARIABLES: for the DIVISION/SBU

WG/J Name of innovative competitor in US/UK	
Established more than 5 years ago (date)	
Numbers of employees (minimum 200)	
Sales turnover	
Real growth in organic sales – annual average over the last three years	
Faster/Same/Slower than industry peers:	

MEETING CONTACTS:
SECTION A:

DATE	NAME	POSITION
_____	_____	_____

SECTION B:

_____	_____	_____

SECTION A – THE DIVISION OR STRATEGIC BUSINESS UNIT

1. Is anyone made responsible specifically for managing the existing product lines – for watching the *profitability* of particular products and for making recommendations for product *deletions*? Do you, for example, have product or brand managers who have these responsibilities? Do you measure product profitability?

2. Do you have a broad product range? How many different products do you sell which you have developed yourself?

3. Can I see a current *organization chart*, or can you outline it to me?* Where does the real power lie as far as product innovation is concerned? Have you experimented with different organizational arrangements?

   i. Has the organization changed recently?
   ii. Do people frequently move from post to post?
   iii. How long do people stay with the company?

   *For overall SPECIALIZATION and overall STRATIFICATION

4. FOR DEFINITIONAL PURPOSES SHOW CLASSIFICATION OF OPTIONS

   1) When was it that you introduced your last new product line developed in-house?

   .... 19...

   2) When do you envisage introducing your next new product line developed in-house?

   19...

   3) Which sort of product innovation activities are you pursuing most vigorously at present?

   4) Do you, or does the holding company, have a new venture group for NPD?

   ## EMPHASIS ON PD AND NPD ACTIVITIES

	PD, PD⁺ and NPD	NNPD ... etc
Markets to which you sell at present:		
New markets to which you do not sell at present:		

CLASSIFICATION OF PRODUCT INNOVATION OPTIONS

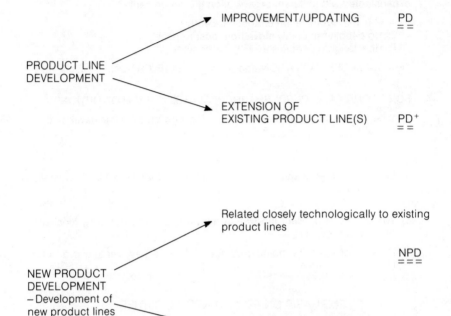

PRODUCT LINE
DEVELOPMENT

IMPROVEMENT/UPDATING $\quad$ PD

EXTENSION OF
EXISTING PRODUCT LINE(S) $\quad$ PD$^+$

NEW PRODUCT
DEVELOPMENT
– Development of
new product lines

Related closely technologically to existing
product lines

NPD

Not related closely technologically to
existing product lines

NNPD

5. What type of *formal meetings* are held to discuss product innovation matters?
   Where does the real power lie for product innovation activities?

STRATEGIC ISSUES	TACTICAL ISSUES

6. Of the two types of new product development, how many projects do you
   have on the go at any one time? (Enter on question 11)

7. What typically happens? Is a rigorous set of steps followed?

8. Roughly what percentage of *time* do the heads of functions spend on product innovation matters (as opposed to running the existing business)?

Chief executive	...%
Technical head	...%
Manufacturing head	...%
Marketing head	...%
....	...%

9. What *length of commercial life* do you anticipate from a new product line introduced on to the market now? I am asking this question to get a feel for how turbulent your market is.

    ....years

10. Would you undertake product developments in anticipation of *customer demand* or in response to it? I am asking the question to get a feel for whether you or your customers determine the sort of new products to develop. Probe for MAP/CAP.

11. What type and number of new product developments do you have actively on the go at any one time?

NEW PRODUCT DEVELOPMENTS		NEW NEW PRODUCT DEVELOPMENTS	
Number on the go:	—	Number on the go:	—
Average development period:	—	Average development period:	—
Average number completed each year	...	Average number completed each year	...
Average unit development cost	...	Average unit development cost	...

12. For what level of anticipated total project expenditure do you prepare a systematic expenditure proposal? And when is it drawn up?

    ....

13. How is Research and Engineering expenditure split between:
    i. Process Innovation
    ii. Product Innovation
    iii. Advanced Engineering (Research)

		OWN	CONTRACT	
i *PROCESS INNOVATION*	%			100%
ii *PRODUCT INNOVATION*	%			100%
iii *ADVANCED ENGINEERING* (Research)	%			100%
	100%			

14.1 Without going into commercially sensitive details, is there an explicit strategy or *plan* underpinning the type of NPD you do? Is it written or spoken predominantly?   (TS)–C

5	4	3	2	1
Explicit : written				Implicit

14.2 What time horizon is used for allocating monies for NPD? (TS)–S

5	4	3	2	1
Years				Years

15.1 Have *procedures* been established for NPD planning purposes? (ST) If so, are these:

Described in detail in an operating manual	5
Outlined in guidesheets or checklists	4
Built up on the basis of written precedent	3
Built up on the basis of the spoken word	2
None	1

15.2 Generally are there a lot of standardized procedures in the division? (Overall STANDARDIZATION)

5	4	3	2	1
A lot				Relatively few

16.   How closely are procedures adhered to in preparing NPD plans?   (SC)

Very closely	5
Closely	4
Quite closely	3
Loosely	2
Not at all/not applicable	1

17.   How much direct influence does the CE have in formulating the NPD strategy?   (CC)

Very much	5
Quite a lot	4
To some extent	3
A little	2
None	1

18.   Generally, does the CEO exercise a hands-on approach in running the division?   (OVERALL CENTRALIZATION)

5	4	3	2	1
Hands-on				Hands-off

19. Which departments (or functions) are involved directly in NPD planning in order of importance (FS) and at which level?

	Corporate Level	Policy Level	Senior Man.	Middle Man.	Junior Man.
1......	5	4	3	2	1
2......	5	4	3	2	1
3......	5	4	3	2	1
4......	5	4	3	2	1
5......	5	4	3	2	1

20. Ring the level within departments with the greatest influence in this activity. (CD)

	Corporate Level	Policy Level	Senior Man.	Middle Man.	Junior Man.
1......	5	4	3	2	1
2......	5	4	3	2	1
3......	5	4	3	2	1
4......	5	4	3	2	1
5......	5	4	3	2	1

21. How frequently, on average, are *formal interdepartmental meetings* held to discuss and review NP strategic issues as a separate item on the agenda? INDICATE FOR EVERY LEVEL AT WHICH THESE OCCUR (FM) (this refers back to question 5)

	Corporate Level	Policy Level	Senior Man.	Middle Man.	Junior Man.
Weekly	5	5	5	5	5
Monthly	4	4	4	4	4
Quarterly	3	3	3	3	3
Annually	2	2	2	2	2
None	1	1	1	1	1

22.1. Is the NPD strategy communicated to those affected by it predominantly in *writing* or by use of the spoken word? (FC)

Predominantly in writing	5
More in writing than spoken	4
About equal	3
More spoken than written	2
Predominantly spoken	1

22.2. Generally is there a lot of *written confirmation* of decisions in the division, or is the spoken word used predominantly?
(OVERALL FORMALIZATION)

5	4	3	2	1
Predominantly written				Predominantly spoken

23. How fast is the pace of change in the *technology* on which your and your competitors' products developments are based?

5	4	3	2	1
Very fast		Medium		Slow

24. Do you undertake product innovation for a global market or mainly for a local market?

5	4	3	2	1
Global Market				Local Market

25. What percentage of your turnover is exported or traded internationally? (Average over the last three years)

...%

26. Now a slightly cheeky question. In general terms is your firm among the *leaders* or among the *followers* in the three types of product innovation?

PD, PD⁺ →	5	4	3	2	1
	Leader	Fast Second	Challenger	Follower	Defender
NPD →5		4	3	2	1
NNPD →5		4	3	2	1

27. Approximately what percentage of your current sales revenues comes from products updated or newly created in the last 5 years? What is the split?

    i. PRODUCT DEVELOPMENTS (IMPROVEMENTS)   ...%

    ii. NEW PRODUCT DEVELOPMENT   ...%   } ...%

    iii. NEW NEW PRODUCT DEVELOPMENTS   ...%

                                      100%

28. What are your development times? Are you normally:

5	4	3	2	1
Faster		About Same		Slower

than your world competitors?

29. Do you contribute to funding central R&D efforts, or are you on your own as far as product innovation is concerned?

    ... What amounts of money can be spent without referring to the corporate centre?

30. What percentage of turnover has been spent over the last three years on average per year on R&D?   ...%

31. Do you consider your company offers sufficient carrots to encourage individuals to push ahead actively with new products?

32. What training do you give your staff in this area?

SECTION B – THE TASK GROUP WITHIN THE UNIT OF ANALYSIS

2.1 What percentage of managers are over 45?
($\frac{1}{2}$ term point in an average managerial
career spanning 40 years) ...%

2.2 Have you used product development agencies, or any other agencies to help out with product development?

2.3 We have identified 4 different types of product innovation For the types you engage in is the development process managed in basically the same way for each type, or are there important differences in approach?

2.4 Indicate the type of product innovation scored in Section B.

      PD ......
      PD$^+$ ......
      NPD ......
      NNPD ......

COLLECTION OF IDEAS

1(a) Do you focus the search for new product ideas in such a way as to define your potential market quite broadly or quite narrowly?   (TS)–C

5	4	3	2	1
Broad focus				Narrow Focus

1(b) What *specific activities* do you engage in to increase the number of ideas? (Aided recall)   (TS)–S

...	Suggestion scheme	5
...	Specific persons are asked to collect & collate ideas	4
...	Specifically commissioned customer analysis	3
...	Working with pet customers	2
...	Technical forecasting	1
...	Brainstorming-type sessions	

2. Which *department* comes up with most ideas? Which is second? ... third? ... any others?   AND AT WHICH LEVEL?   (FS)

	Corporate Level	Policy Level	Senior Man.	Middle Man.	Junior Man.
1......	5	4	3	2	1
2......	5	4	3	2	1
3......	5	4	3	2	1
4......	5	4	3	2	1
5......	5	4	3	2	1

3. Ring the level(s) within departments with the greatest *influence* in this activity. (CD)

	Corporate Level	Policy Level	Senior Man.	Middle Man.	Junior Man.
1......	5	4	3	2	1
2......	5	4	3	2	1
3......	5	4	3	2	1
4......	5	4	3	2	1
5......	5	4	3	2	1

4. Are any *formal interdepartmental meetings* held where the collection and coordination of ideas occurs as a specific item on the agenda? How frequently, on average, are these held?   INDICATE FOR EVERY LEVEL AT WHICH THESE OCCUR   (FM)

	Corporate Level	Policy Level	Senior Man.	Middle Man.	Junior Man.
Weekly	5	5	5	5	5
Monthly	4	4	4	4	4
Quarterly	3	3	3	3	3
Annually	2	2	2	2	2
None	1	1	1	1	1

INITIAL SCREENING

1(a) Not all ideas can be taken up either in the short or long run. Are ideas ordered purposively so as to select the most appropriate ones?   (TS)–C

5	4	3	2	1
Ideas are ordered in a pool explicitly in writing			Ideas are assessed on an ad hoc basis	

1(b) Are the criteria used for screening quite clear to everyone, i.e. perceived in the same way, or not? ... Are these written down – can I see them? – which are the most important criteria?   LIST THESE   (TS)–S

5	4	3	2	1
Explicit: in writing				Implicit: spoken

What percentage of ideas fall away at this stage?   ...%

2. In order of importance, which *departments* are most involved directly in screening?   AND AT WHICH LEVEL?   (FS)

	Corporate Level	Policy Level	Senior Man.	Middle Man.	Junior Man.
1......	5	4	3	2	1
2......	5	4	3	2	1
3......	5	4	3	2	1
4......	5	4	3	2	1
5......	5	4	3	2	1

3. Ring the level(s) within departments with the greatest *influence* in this activity. (CD)

	Corporate Level	Policy Level	Senior Man.	Middle Man.	Junior Man.
1......	5	4	3	2	1
2......	5	4	3	2	1
3......	5	4	3	2	1
4......	5	4	3	2	1
5......	5	4	3	2	1

4. Are ideas screened at any *formal interdepartmental meetings*? How frequently, on average, do they occur?   INDICATE FOR EVERY LEVEL AT WHICH THESE OCCUR   (FM)

	Corporate Level	Policy Level	Senior Man.	Middle Man.	Junior Man.
Weekly	5	5	5	5	5
Monthly	4	4	4	4	4
Quarterly	3	3	3	3	3
Annually	2	2	2	2	2
None	1	1	1	1	1

INITIAL INVESTIGATION

1(a) Is a sum of money set aside formally for investigating the feasibility of a *specific* idea, or is such investigation undertaken on a less formal basis? (TS)–C Up to how much? ....

5	4	3	2	1
Formal				Informal

1(b) At this stage, what relative emphasis is placed on investigating: (TS)–S

THE COMMERCIAL FEASIBILITY ...%
THE TECHNICAL FEASIBILITY ...%

What percentage of investigated ideas are rejected during this activity? ...%

2. In order of importance, which *departments* are most involved directly in this? AND AT WHICH LEVEL? (FS)

	Corporate Level	Policy Level	Senior Man.	Middle Man.	Junior Man.
1......	5	4	3	2	1
2......	5	4	3	2	1
3......	5	4	3	2	1
4......	5	4	3	2	1
5......	5	4	3	2	1

3. Ring the level(s) within departments with the greatest *influence* in this activity. (CD)

	Corporate Level	Policy Level	Senior Man.	Middle Man.	Junior Man.
1......	5	4	3	2	1
2......	5	4	3	2	1
3......	5	4	3	2	1
4......	5	4	3	2	1
5......	5	4	3	2	1

4. Is progress monitored at any *formal interdepartmental meetings*. How frequently do these occur? INDICATE FOR EVERY LEVEL AT WHICH THESE OCCUR (FM)

	Corporate Level	Policy Level	Senior Man.	Middle Man.	Junior Man.
Weekly	5	5	5	5	5
Monthly	4	4	4	4	4
Quarterly	3	3	3	3	3
Annually	2	2	2	2	2
None	1	1	1	1	1

PRIORITY ANALYSIS/ASSESSMENT

1(a) In some companies concepts which have been investigated initially are evaluated against each other formally on a competitive basis for choosing which ones to develop fully before others (from a pool). Does this happen with you? ... or does the development process tend to run on automatically? (Only score this page if there is a competitive basis for selection)

(TS)–C   NO ☐   YES ☐   ⇨ Score......

5	4	3	2	1
Competitive evaluation: formal (written)			Ad hoc evaluation	

1(b) For the purpose of appraising the potential usefulness of initially investigated business propositions are the criteria used written down – can I see them – which is the most important? (TS)–S

5	4	3	2	1
Explicit: written down			Implicit: spoken	

What percentage of propositions are rejected?   ...%

2. In order of importance, which *departments* are most involved directly in the evaluation?   AND AT WHICH LEVEL?   (FS)

	Corporate Level	Policy Level	Senior Man.	Middle Man.	Junior Man.
1......	5	4	3	2	1
2......	5	4	3	2	1
3......	5	4	3	2	1
4......	5	4	3	2	1
5......	5	4	3	2	1

3. Ring the level(s) within departments with the greatest *influence* in this activity. (CD)

	Corporate Level	Policy Level	Senior Man.	Middle Man.	Junior Man.
1......	5	4	3	2	1
2......	5	4	3	2	1
3......	5	4	3	2	1
4......	5	4	3	2	1
5......	5	4	3	2	1

4. Do you hold *formal interdepartmental meetings* for priority analysis purposes? How frequently, on average, do these occur?   INDICATE FOR EVERY LEVEL AT WHICH THESE OCCUR   (FM)

	Corporate Level	Policy Level	Senior Man.	Middle Man.	Junior Man.
Weekly	5	5	5	5	5
Monthly	4	4	4	4	4
Quarterly	3	3	3	3	3
Annually	2	2	2	2	2
None	1	1	1	1	1

DEVELOPMENT PROPER (INCLUDING PROTOTYPE STAGE)
(FIRMING OF DESIGN, PRODUCTION FACILITIES & MARKETING PLAN)

1(a) How is a product development tracked?   (TS)–C

Probe for whether a team is formally appointed with a team leader to look after the development (HIGH = 5) or whether the task is left to happen within the organization as a whole (LOW = 5).

1(b) Are any specific control techniques used for monitoring progress? (TS)–S   Unaided recall:

> **What percentage of developments are stopped (i) MIDSTREAM** ...%
>
> **and (ii) END OF DEVELOPMENT** ...%

2. In order of importance, which *departments* are most involved directly in this? AND AT WHICH LEVEL? (FS)

	Corporate Level	Policy Level	Senior Man.	Middle Man.	Junior Man.
1......	5	4	3	2	1
2......	5	4	3	2	1
3......	5	4	3	2	1
4......	5	4	3	2	1
5......	5	4	3	2	1

3. Ring the level(s) within departments with the greatest *influence* in this activity. (CD)

	Corporate Level	Policy Level	Senior Man.	Middle Man.	Junior Man.
1......	5	4	3	2	1
2......	5	4	3	2	1
3......	5	4	3	2	1
4......	5	4	3	2	1
5......	5	4	3	2	1

4. Is progress monitored at any *formal interdepartmental meetings* which could stop the development? How frequently do these occur? INDICATE FOR EVERY LEVEL AT WHICH THESE OCCUR (FM)

	Corporate Level	Policy Level	Senior Man.	Middle Man.	Junior Man.
Weekly	5	5	5	5	5
Monthly	4	4	4	4	4
Quarterly	3	3	3	3	3
Annually	2	2	2	2	2
None	1	1	1	1	1

CAPITAL SANCTION

1(a) Are capital projects chosen from a pool of possible projects? (TS)–C

YES ☐   NO ☐

1(b) List the appraisal techniques used (unaided recall). (TS)–S

5
4
3
2
1

What percentage of developed products are rejected at the capital sanction stage? ...%

2. In order of importance, which *departments* are most involved directly in preparing the proposal?   AND AT WHICH LEVEL?   (FS)

	Corporate Level	Policy Level	Senior Man.	Middle Man.	Junior Man.
1......	5	4	3	2	1
2......	5	4	3	2	1
3......	5	4	3	2	1
4......	5	4	3	2	1
5......	5	4	3	2	1

3. Ring the level(s) within departments with the greatest *influence* in this activity. (CD)

	Corporate Level	Policy Level	Senior Man.	Middle Man.	Junior Man.
1......	5	4	3	2	1
2......	5	4	3	2	1
3......	5	4	3	2	1
4......	5	4	3	2	1
5......	5	4	3	2	1

4. Are proposals considered at any *formal interdepartmental meetings*? How frequently, on average, do these occur?   INDICATE FOR EVERY LEVEL AT WHICH THESE OCCUR   (FM)

	Corporate Level	Policy Level	Senior Man.	Middle Man.	Junior Man.
Weekly	5	5	5	5	5
Monthly	4	4	4	4	4
Quarterly	3	3	3	3	3
Annually	2	2	2	2	2
None	1	1	1	1	1

LAUNCH   (INCLUDING FORMAL TEST MARKET)

1(a) Do you prepare an explicit plan for launch purposes?   (TS)–C

5	4	3	2	1
Explicit: written				Implicit

1(b) Do you launch usually on a national or on an international basis?   (TS)–S

5	4	3	2	1
International				National

What is the failure rate in terms of meeting the originally envisaged objectives?   ...%

2.   In order of importance, which *departments* are most involved directly in this?   AND AT WHICH LEVEL?   (FS)

	Corporate Level	Policy Level	Senior Man.	Middle Man.	Junior Man.
1......	5	4	3	2	1
2......	5	4	3	2	1
3......	5	4	3	2	1
4......	5	4	3	2	1
5......	5	4	3	2	1

3.   Ring the level(s) within departments with the greatest *influence* in this activity. (CD)

	Corporate Level	Policy Level	Senior Man.	Middle Man.	Junior Man.
1......	5	4	3	2	1
2......	5	4	3	2	1
3......	5	4	3	2	1
4......	5	4	3	2	1
5......	5	4	3	2	1

4.   How frequently, on average, are *formal interdepartmental meetings* held to monitor launch details?   INDICATE FOR EVERY LEVEL AT WHICH THESE OCCUR   (FM)

	Corporate Level	Policy Level	Senior Man.	Middle Man.	Junior Man.
Weekly	5	5	5	5	5
Monthly	4	4	4	4	4
Quarterly	3	3	3	3	3
Annually	2	2	2	2	2
None	1	1	1	1	1

INFLUENCE OF THE CEO (CC)

How much does the CEO (of the unit of analysis) involve himself directly in the activities?

	He takes control	He watches very closely indeed	He takes a genuine interest	He is involved indirectly	None
	5	4	3	2	1
Collection of ideas					
Initial screening					
Initial investigation					
Priority analysis/assessment					
Product development proper					
Capital sanction					
Launch (formal test market)					

STANDARDIZED PROCEDURES   (ST)

Have any standardized procedures been established for undertaking the activities?

	Described in detail in an operating manual	Outlined in checklists or guide-sheets	Built up on the basis of written precedent	Built up on the basis of the spoken word	None
	5	4	3	2	1
Collection of ideas					
Initial screening					
Initial investigation					
Priority analysis/assessment					
Product development proper					
Capital sanction					
Launch (formal test market)					

HOW CLOSELY ARE THESE NORMALLY ADHERED TO   (SC)

	Very closely	Closely	Quite closely	Loosely	Not at all/None
	5	4	3	2	1
Collection of ideas					
Initial screening					
Initial investigation					
Priority analysis/assessment					
Product development proper					
Capital sanction					
Launch (formal test market)					

FORMAL COMMUNICATION   (FC)

To what extent is communication during each activity in writing as opposed to being spoken?

	Predomi-nantly in writing	More in writing than spoken	About equal	More spoken than written	Predomi-nantly spoken
	5	4	3	2	1
Collection of ideas					
Initial screening					
Initial investigation					
Priority analysis/assessment					
Product development proper					
Capital sanction					
Launch (formal test market)					

FINALLY

i Do you consider top management in your firm gives the support needed to achieve speedy and efficient NPD?

ii Do you consider there are sufficient inducements for staff to take the personal risks associated with product development activities?

Appendix 2: Management Check-list

Based on the analytical schema in chapter 3.

I YOUR TOP MANAGEMENT APPROACH TO PRODUCT DEVELOPMENT

I STRATEGY

1.1 Does long-term profitability drive your firm (as opposed to an overriding emphasis on short-term financial results)?

Yes ☐   No ☐

1.2 Is the product development strategy spelled out in writing, and does it explain in detail the contributions expected from different types of product developments (product improvements and new product developments) over the next years?

Yes ☐   No ☐

1.3 Does your promotional literature contain a clause like: 'Due to our policy of continuous product development we will, when appropriate, alter design/construction in the best interests of our customers'?

Yes ☐   No ☐

1.4 Does your firm possess strong brand names under which new products can be launched?

Yes ☐   No ☐

YOUR TOP MANAGEMENT APPROACH TO PRODUCT DEVELOPMENT

2   STRUCTURE

2.1 Is your firm organized on a business basis (as opposed to a structure based primarily on products or functions)?

Yes ☐   No ☐

2.2 Are clear lines of responsibility laid down for product developments? Specifically, is it always clear who is ultimately responsible for different types of product developments?

Yes ☐   No ☐

2.3 Are there individuals in the firm, either self-selected or assigned, who regularly initiate and push along product developments?

Yes ☐   No ☐

2.4 Is there clear evidence of formally established interfunctional teams for pursuing different types of product developments?

Yes ☐   No ☐

YOUR TOP MANAGEMENT APPROACH TO PRODUCT DEVELOPMENT

3 SHARED VALUES

3.1 Does top management provide consistent and visible commitment of funds and resources for product developments? The important word here is *consistent*: it is not sufficient to commit resources on a purely sporadic basis.

Yes ☐ No ☐

3.2 Are both senior and junior persons routinely involved in product development tasks *throughout* the whole process?

Yes ☐ No ☐

3.3 Are there compensation programs in place to encourage individuals to participate in development work *throughout* the whole process?

Yes ☐ No ☐

3.4 Is the strategy for product development consistently and regularly communicated to all involved?

Yes ☐ No ☐

YOUR TOP MANAGEMENT APPROACH TO PRODUCT DEVELOPMENT

4 STYLE

4.1 Is top management willing to take ultimate responsibility for individual product developments? Specifically, is top management prepared to accept product development failures?

Yes ☐   No ☐

4.2 Does top management explain, on a regular ongoing basis, to the whole organization the role which new products are expected to play and the contributions expected from different persons?

Yes ☐   No ☐

4.3 Is top management approval of and continuing support for product developments guided by a common set of criteria (as opposed to using *ad hoc* criteria)?

Yes ☐   No ☐

II *YOUR TEAMWORK PRACTICES FOR PRODUCT DEVELOPMENT*

5 STAFF

5.1 Are developments attended to as a team effort with marketing and technical matters being addressed simultaneously (as opposed to being the responsibility of one main function)?

Yes ☐ No ☐

5.2 Are project teams staffed with persons who have good inter-personal skills and who are capable of rising above functional allegiances?

Yes ☐ No ☐

5.3 Are project team leaders chosen for their ability to combine functional skills and to administer complex tasks?

Yes ☐ No ☐

YOUR TEAMWORK PRACTICES FOR PRODUCT DEVELOPMENT

6   SKILLS

6.1 Do suggestions for possible product developments come primarily from a consideration of market-related factors (as opposed to an overriding consideration of supply-side factors)?

Yes ☐   No ☐

6.2 Are marketing and technical staff provided with formal *and* regular training on product development matters?

Yes ☐   No ☐

6.3 Are formal financial and strategic screening procedures used to evaluate suggestions for product developments *and* do these screens take account of differences in the degrees of risk associated with different types of propositions?

Yes ☐   No ☐

6.4 Does evaluation continue *throughout* the product development process?

Yes ☐   No ☐

YOUR TEAMWORK PRACTICES FOR PRODUCT DEVELOPMENT

7 SYSTEMS

7.1 Is there a clearly laid down and adhered to go/no go approval process for monitoring product development progress from inception to launch?

Yes ☐ No ☐

7.2 Is product development performance formally monitored after launch and tracked against original project objectives?

Yes ☐ No ☐

7.3 Is there evidence of a loose–tight mode of operation (as opposed to control and co-ordination being predominantly loose *or* tight)?

Yes ☐ No ☐

7.4 If speedy product development is important, have you recently reviewed your development procedures?

Yes ☐ No ☐

Additional Reading

All these books provide a rewarding and thought-provoking message that is directly useful for business purposes.

Abegglen, J. C. and Stalk, G. (1985) *Kaisha, the Japanese Corporation*. New York: Basic Books.
A revised and updated edition of Ansoff's classic on strategy, including discussions on incremental as opposed to discontinuous change, and growth through organic product development as opposed to growth through acquisition.

Ansoff, H. I. (1987) *Corporate Strategy* (Revised edition). London: Penguin.
A revised and updated edition of Ansoff's classic on strategy, including discussions on incremental as opposed to discontinuous change, and growth through organic product development as opposed to growth through acquisition.

Bergen, S. A. (1986) *Project Management*. Oxford: Basil Blackwell.
A practical book dealing with topics such as project selection, project planning, organization and control, motivation of project teams.

Bobrow, E. E. and Shafer, D. W. (1987) *Pioneering New Products*. Homewood, IL: Dow Jones–Irwin.
A practical step-by-step guide to the process of developing and marketing new products. Sections on brainstorming, attribute listing, morphological analysis, synectics, concept screening, etc.

Booz, Allen & Hamilton (1982) *New Products Management for the 1980s*. New York: Booz, Allen & Hamilton.
Suggests that good product development practice will follow an orderly set of steps consisting of: (1) new product planning, (2) idea generation, (3) screening, (4) concept development, (5) business analysis, (6) product development, (7) test marketing, (8) launch. Best practice is found to be: well-defined NPD strategy, flexible organization, supportive top management, and high resource allocation early in the NPD process.

Botkin, J., Dimancescu, D. and Stata, R. (1986) *The Innovators: Rediscovering America's Creative Energy*. Philadelphia: University of Pennsylvania Press.
The authors argue that truly important innovations are those which change the basis of competition (i.e. marketing and distribution systems), disrupt production competences, and threaten organization structures.

Burgelman, R. A. and Sayles, L. R. (1986) *Inside Corporate Innovation: Strategy,*

Structure and Managerial Skills. New York: Free Press.

The authors argue that the challenge for established firms is to be able to live with and manage the tensions generated between a well-organized management approach on the one hand, and a potentially disruptive approach to exploiting new opportunities on the other.

Cooper, R. G. (1986) *Winning at New Products*. Toronto: Holt, Rinehart & Winston.

Written for the practising manager, this book is based on the author's extensive researches in Canadian firms.

Crawford, C. M. (1987) *New Products Management* (2nd edn). Homewood, IL: Irwin.

Excellent standard textbook on new product development which is suitable for all students of the subject.

Davidson, H. (1987) *Offensive Marketing or How to make your Competitors Followers* (2nd edn). London: Penguin.

Argues that too many companies meekly follow the lead of their competitors, producing feeble 'me-too' products in a vain attempt to catch up. To succeed in the long run they should counterattack, using POISE – marketing that is Profitable, Offensive, Integrated, Strategic and Effectively executed.

Foster, R. N. (1986) *Innovation: The Attacker's Advantage*. London: Macmillan.

Shows that past leaders can become losers by clinging to old technology for too long: their past success in the marketplace blinds them to new technical change which is therefore often applied first by other industries.

Freeman, C. (1982) *The Economics of Industrial Innovation* (2nd edn). London: Francis Pinter.

Contains details of the SAPPHO study's findings.

Gardiner, P. and Rothwell, R. (1985) *Innovation: A Study of the Problems and Benefits of Product Innovation*. London: Design Council.

Useful pamphlet with British case studies and references.

Ginzberg, E. and Vojta, G. (1985) *Beyond Human Scale: The Large Corporation at Risk*. New York: Basic Books.

Argues that the large corporation is an endangered species, although it remains a dominant business institution. Demonstrates that the increasing scale and complexity of the large corporation leads to the under-utilization of management personnel who spend time and energy on co-ordinating and internal politics rather than on the important task of making better and more profitable products.

Goold, M. and Campbell, A. (1987) *Strategies and Styles: The Role of the Centre in Managing Diversified Corporations*. Oxford: Basil Blackwell.

Based on a study of 16 leading British-based multinationals the book examines the relationship between corporate, divisional and business units in the management of change. Identifies eight distinct management styles of which three are particularly common: (1) strategic planning ('orchestrating'), (2) strategic control ('coaching'), (3) financial control.

Hippel, E. von (1988) *The Sources of Innovation*. Oxford: Oxford University Press.

Explains how many innovations are suggested to manufacturers by their customers. Includes substantial case history material.

Holt, K. (1988) *Product Innovation Management: Workbook for Management in Industry* (3rd edn). London: Butterworth.

Reference book on innovation and product development which provides detailed explanations of techniques such as Delphi, brainstorming, synectics, cross-impact analysis, forecasting, project management, test marketing and product planning.

Johne, F. A. (1985) *Industrial Product Innovation*. New York: Nichols.

Examines the hypothesis that loose co-ordination and control systems are conducive to initiating product developments but that tight systems are needed to implement developments successfully. Provides case study material from British and American electronics firms.

Johnson, G. (1987) *Strategic Change and the Management Process*. Oxford: Basil Blackwell.

Examines strategic change in an old-established British clothing manufacturing firm. Shows how strategic change in such a firm is critically dependent on management's skill rather than on brilliant rational analysis. This is because long-serving managers commonly resist views or actions which diverge from currently held beliefs, even when disaster is staring them in the face.

Kraushar, P. (1985) *Practical Business Development*. London: Holt, Rinehart & Winston.

Makes a clear distinction between old product development, new product development and new business development, and the factors contributing to success in each.

Kuczmarski, T. D. (1988) *Managing New Products*. Englewood Cliffs, New Jersey: Prentice Hall.

By the leader of the Booz, Allen & Hamilton 1982 study (see above). Provides practical advice on how companies can increase their success rate in launching new products. Argues that the biggest obstacle to new product success is management's emphasis on short-term profitability, and that large corporations need to learn from small start-up businesses.

Lloyd, T. (1986) *Dinosaur & Co. Studies in Corporate Evolution*. London: Penguin.

Argues that small, high-technology companies are emerging to show the way forward in organizational structuring for the future.

O'Hare, M. (1988) *Innovate! How to Gain and Sustain Competitive Advantage*. Oxford: Basil Blackwell.

Argues that firms can thrive in the new business age if they learn to innovate strategically. Shows how this can be done by achieving synergy between the value chains of suppliers, manufacturers and customers. Too many firms still focus on individual innovations at the expense of this form of broader innovativeness.

Ohmae, K. (1982) *The Mind of the Strategist: Business Planning for Competitive Advantage*. London: Penguin.

Argues on the basis of examples from Japanese firms such as Sony, Nissan, Honda and Yamaha that strategic analysis is the key to business success. Suggests that firms should conceptually think in terms of 'strategic planning units' which act as the interpreters of changing market requirements to be exploited by Strategic Business Units.

Parkinson, S. T. (1984) *New Product Development in Engineering*. Cambridge: Cambridge University Press.

Argues the thesis that an industry's local market will critically affect its marketing ability and, specifically, Britain's small insular market has detrimentally affected its machine tool industry.

Pascale, R. T. and Athos, A. G. (1982) *The Art of Japanese Management*. London: Penguin Books.

Looks closely at Matsushita and argues that a co-ordinated productive interdependence in approach allows it to achieve results which are superior to those of Western firms that rely on potentially disruptive individualism. Suggests that Western firms should consider creating a managerial system which draws strength from both approaches.

Peters, T. J. and Waterman, R. H. (1982) *In Search of Excellence: Lessons from America's Best-run Companies*. New York: Harper & Row.

Explains the 7Ss framework for analysing firms (two hard Ss: strategy and structure; five soft Ss: style, systems, staff, skills, shared values). Argues that leading firms distinguish themselves on eight factors: (1) bias for action, (2) close to the customer, (3) autonomy and entrepreneurship, (4) productivity through people, (5) hands-on, value-driven, (6) stick to the knitting, (7) simple form, lean staff, (8) simultaneous loose–tight properties.

Pilditch, J. (1987) *Winning Ways*. London: Harper & Row.

Excellently argued book: full of insight and inspiration on how 'winning' companies create new products.

Pinchot, G. (1985) *Intrapreneuring: Why you don't have to leave the Corporation to become an Entrepreneur*. New York: Harper & Row.

Arguably one of the most liberating concepts to have emerged in recent years. Like entrepreneurs, intrapreneurs are in the grip of a great idea which, when given the freedom and incentive of a private venture and the resources of a large company, can result in highly successful new products.

Souder, W. E. (1987) *Managing New Product Innovations*. Lexington, MA: D. C. Heath.

Examines life cycle data from nearly 300 new product innovations over a ten year period. Argues that systematic approaches are more successful. Advances ten principles of good new product management: (1) special management qualities, (2) great patience, (3) don't try to use traditional budget techniques, (4) don't use classical organizational approaches, (5) select projects systematically, (6) manage projects in a cost-effective way, (7) eliminate disharmony between R&D and marketing, (8) analyse the customer's level of product sophistication and your level of technical sophistication, (9) use resources appropriate to the technology being used, (10) pay close attention to internal technology transfers.

Index

Note: Italics indicate pages with tables or figures